ENCOUNTER IN THE CLASSROOM

New Ways of Teaching

ELIZABETH HUNTER
Hunter College, City University of New York

HOLT, RINEHART AND WINSTON, INC.
New York   Chicago   San Francisco   Atlanta
Dallas   Montreal   Toronto   London   Sydney

My association as a network member of the NTL Institute for Applied Behavioral Science has helped me immeasurably in the writing of this book. The NTL Institute, an independent organization associated with the National Education Association, utilizes the laboratory method of learning (learning from studying one's own behavior, the behavior of others, and interactive behavior during various individual and group activities) in order to bring about constructive personal and organizational change.

Preface

There is much talk about the need for change in education and, indeed, there are currently many attempts at bringing about change. However, most of these attempts involve the structure or content of education rather than the process, that is, the interaction of people in the schools. It is the thesis of this book that process—and teaching *is* process—is the area where modification must occur if schools are to change in any important way.

Students are clamoring for 'relevance,' 'engagement,' and

'participation' in their classes, and teachers would like to provide these qualities, but in many cases neither group knows how to achieve them. *Encounter in the Classroom* contains a large number of activities for classroom use that will provide the involvement so desperately sought and needed for improved learning. This book is designed to bring about constructive change in the professional education courses of colleges and universities, and in the schools with children.

Activities are included which will help you to use encounter and sensitivity group techniques for increasing personal and interpersonal effectiveness. There are also skill sessions for analyzing and improving classroom talk, for improving the quality of classroom questions, and for helping teachers work more harmoniously with other adults. Thus, the teacher training classroom can actually serve as a model for the kind of participatory learning, which, though frequently advocated in education courses, is often ignored in practice. After suggested modifications, many of the activities may be used with children, and Chapter 6 describes a fifth grade classroom in which the teacher is implementing some new ways of teaching.

This text is intended for undergraduate and graduate courses that focus upon the teaching process, whether they be psychology or methods courses, and will be useful for students who are currently working in schools, as well as for teachers in the field. In addition, since the book provides for many direct teaching and learning experiences in the college classroom, it will be helpful in courses where students have no immediate contact with youngsters, yet are eager for encounters with new ways of teaching.

Elizabeth Hunter

New York City
August 1971

Contents

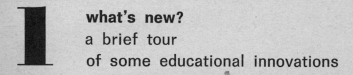

1   what's new?
a brief tour
of some educational innovations

Let us begin by touring a number of schools which have adopted innovations current in American education. The incidents presented on this tour are all too real; only the names have been changed to protect the guilty.

Nongraded Classrooms

Blair, a child in the nongraded primary, stumbles along with his reading, as usual. He knows that he isn't doing well, and he knows that he has missed the same words before. He waits with bowed head for the criticism, and it comes as expected. "Blair, I don't know what I'm going to do with you. You've been in this section for a year and a half already, but it looks as if you'll be here for another year. If you don't try harder, I don't know how you're ever going to learn to read. Now, Ralph, you take a turn, and Blair, *you* pay attention."

> **Moral:**   What we call the class won't matter to a child who isn't learning. No name will be sweet.

The Extended Day

The committee in charge of planning and putting into effect the extended day in the Bond School is having a heated discussion about the results of the first four months of the program. "When we made our plans last year," says Mr. Phillips, the principal, "we knew that everything would not go smoothly in the beginning, but I think we have to give this program a chance."

"We aren't objecting to giving the program a chance—we are objecting to the way the program is set up," replies Mr. Bond, one of the teachers. "This was supposed to be an experimental program, which means doing something different, as far as I'm concerned. And we don't really do anything different except keep the kids two hours longer in the afternoon and give them a snack at the time when they used to go home. And since many of our children were not exactly overjoyed with the curriculum in our school to begin with, adding two hours to each day causes many, many problems."

"I have to go along with that," Mr. Mayfair, another teacher, joins in. "We're still following the same inappropriate curriculum bulletins that we followed before, and to make matters worse, we have so many new teachers without previous teaching experience that things are becoming chaotic, especially in the late afternoon."

"What we're saying, Mr. Phillips," adds Mrs. Greene, a committee member from the community, "is that we don't particularly want to give *this* program much more of a chance. The parents are complaining that their children are coming home tired and cranky, and then they have homework to do—after being in school from 8:30 in the morning till 5:00 in the afternoon. Now it seems like the teachers would have enough time to teach them plenty in all those hours without sending work home besides!"

"And that's another thing," Mr. Mayfair speaks again. "Look at most of the homework that's given out in this school. It certainly isn't designed to make kids interested in learning."

"I say let's work on revitalizing the regular school day and throw out these extra hours, which are just making everything worse," Mrs. Brand speaks heatedly.

"Now wait just a minute," replies Mr. Phillips. "We were selected as a model school for this program and I accepted, and everyone said we'd give it a try. Now we just aren't going to throw the whole thing out the window!"

Moral: More is sometimes less.

The New Math

The first grade is working on sets, and Miss Lane has been asking the children to name members of varying kinds of sets. The children, confused by her explanations, make many errors. "I don't know what I'm going to do with this class," frowns Miss Lane. "We've gone over this now for several days, but a lot of you still don't seem to know what I'm talking about. If you can't do these simple kinds of things, what are you going to do next year when the work will be much harder? Math is very important, so listen again while I explain it once more. Remember, I told you that sets are groups of things called members. Every set has members. And when we match the members of one set to the members of another set we call that one-to-one correspondence. Now, I have here a group, I mean a set, of triangles. Joey, don't call out the number please! I'm not interested in that. Now, under the first set I have a group of squares. Children! I asked you not to tell me how many. We aren't concerned about that yet, so there's no need to try to show off. Now, which are the members of these sets? Or, to put it another way, what is in these sets? . . . Well, doesn't anybody know? We've gone over this so many times, I don't know why you can't answer these simple questions!"

> **Moral:** New math taught ineffectively doesn't add up to much.

Team Teaching

Ninety-two children and four teachers working together as a team constitute the fourth grade in the Wilson School. The group has four rooms for its use—one large enough to hold everyone and the other three able to accommodate about twenty-five pupils. On the day of our visit, Mr. Johnson, the team teacher whose specialty is science, is conducting experiments before the entire group. The children watch intently, as they would watch a magic show, for, to them, Mr. Johnson is a magician and science is not really different from magic. Mr. Johnson always makes sure that he provides plenty of drama—explosions, color-changing liquids, and collapsing gallon cans.

"Today I showed you that you can't rely on your hunches," Mr. Johnson summarizes. "What you thought was going to happen wasn't what actually did happen. You saw five demonstrations which proved exactly that. Now, you have cooperated well by sitting quietly and paying close attention, and it's time to break up into our four science groups and work on pages 82 to 85 in the science workbooks. If you have any questions about these pages, your group teacher will help you. Let's move quickly to our separate rooms, beginning with row one."

Moral: Adding teachers to the classroom doesn't necessarily increase the amount of pupil learning.

Sex Education

"Well, now, I believe everyone in the class has had a chance to read aloud from our chapter on reproduction," says Mrs. James to her fifth grade class. "Let's have a few review questions before we go on to spelling. Billy, will you tell us again the definition of osmosis?"

Moral: With very little effort sex education can be taught in as routine a manner as spelling.

Paraprofessionals

Clinton School has people from the community working as paraprofessionals in each grade, helping the regular classroom teachers. Mrs. O'Neil, a middle-aged woman with a large family of her own and two years of experience as an aide, works with Miss Smith, a young beginning teacher.

Miss Smith is standing in front of the sixth grade class teaching a lesson in health; Mrs. O'Neil sits at a desk to one side, correcting papers. The youngsters become restless, as often happens during the day, and invariably during health lessons. Miss Smith faithfully follows the curriculum outlined in the city guide, but somehow it always seems boring, even to Miss Smith. Several pairs of children are whispering, some are daydreaming, and others are fiddling with things on their desks.

"Some of you aren't listening as carefully as you should be," admonishes Miss Smith, "and you won't know this material. Now, let's have everyone paying attention. Jimmy, what does the word 'contagious' mean?"

Jimmy, who is looking out the window completely engrossed in a daydream, doesn't hear Miss Smith speak to him, and when several children begin to giggle, Mrs. O'Neil bellows from the sidelines, "You children heard what Miss Smith said! She said pay attention and she means pay attention. Now, I'm watching all of you, and I'm starting a list right now. Anyone whose name is on the list will stay after school and do extra work. I saw that face you made, Andrea! Just for that your name is the first one on the list, Miss Smartie! Anybody else want to stay after school?"

Miss Smith doesn't really approve of this technique, but she doesn't know what to say, and besides, Mrs. O'Neil is so much older and more experienced than she—and so formidable!

> **Moral:** In some classrooms a scorecard is needed to tell the paras from the pros.

Black History

Mr. Harris is speaking to his class of high school juniors about today's test on their Black history unit. "Let's take a few minutes to go over the test, class. The first question asks you to match the names in the left-hand column with the dates in the right—for example, what was the date of Booker T. Washington's birth? the year the NAACP was founded? and so on. The second question requires you to fill in the answers, and they are to be brief, as you can see. The first one says, '*The Souls of Black Folk* was written by _____.' I think all of those are clear enough. The last question is longer, and asks, 'What was the Supreme Court decision in the Plessy vs. Ferguson case? what year was this decision written? and what later Supreme Court decision countermanded it?' All right, now, you have forty minutes, so let's get started."

> **Moral:** Even Black history can be presented in a colorless manner.

Ability Grouping

Mr. Horn is scolding his class of intellectually gifted eighth graders. "I'm very disappointed in the way you've done this assignment. Just because you people know that you have high IQ's, you think you don't have to do any work, and you're getting more and more careless. Each of you was supposed to list the major exports and imports of the countries you selected, so that we could share these facts with each other. I let you select your own countries, so they would be ones that interested you, but only about one third of you are prepared. If you don't do your work it really doesn't matter how smart you think you are—you won't know things that are important for every educated person to know. Those of you who aren't prepared can stay here during club time and make your lists while I watch. Not very grown-up punishment, I grant you, but suitable for this class!"

Down the hall, Miss Hardart is chastising the slowest group of eighth graders. "Class, you certainly haven't done very well with this assignment. It was simple enough—listing the major exports and imports of the countries we're studying. When I see the way you do your work, it's no surprise to me that you're in the bottom group of eighth graders. You don't even try! I've told you over and over again that achievement is 10 percent inspiration and 90 percent perspiration—which means that if you would only try harder and do more, you would get somewhere. Now, take out your books and do your assignments, and do them correctly. Those few of you who *have* done your work can read ahead for tonight's homework assignment."

Moral: Some teachers dull the gifted while others withhold gifts from the dull.

Programmed Instruction

Miss Brown's second grade in the Gant School is included in a new program involving the use of computers for math. This is the first day the children will be using the machines, and they are excited about what lies ahead. Half of the class at a time goes to a special room where there are fifteen typewriterlike machines which are connected to a large computer many miles away.

Danny Morrow is as thrilled as everyone else. Imagine having the chance to use these machines! He sits down and an instructor shows the children how to turn on the machines. Danny's machine types out the first message: "Hello. What is your name?"

Danny smiles and searches among the keys to answer: "Danny Morrow."

"Wrong," clicks out the machine, to Danny's chagrin. "Try again. What is your name?"

Again Danny types his name into the machine. Again he is told, "Wrong. Try again. What is your name?" This time Danny raises his hand, but the instructor is busy with someone else, so Danny keeps typing, "Danny Morrow," and the machine keeps responding, "Wrong. Try again. What is your name?" From time to time Danny tries to get the instructor's attention, but he never succeeds.

Miss Brown, his teacher, walks into the room to see how things are going and stops first at Danny's side. She sees the foot and a half of paper sticking out of his machine, all covered with the same question and the same answer, and stifles a desire to laugh only because of poor Danny's worried expression. "Well, you seem to be having some trouble here. You know what—I bet the machine thinks your name is Daniel. Try that."

So Danny typed "Daniel Morrow," and the machine typed, "Correct. Now write the missing number in this example. $2 + \square = 4$."

But before Danny could type anything, the period ended and the machine clicked, "Your percentage of correct answers is 0." Fortunately, Danny didn't understand what that meant.

Moral: Machines have a lot to learn, including a guy's nickname.

New Reading Programs

The first grade teachers at the Fraser School are discussing their new reading program during the first hour of their January staff meeting. The Triple L (Look, Listen, Learn) Program was being used in all the first grades that year, and the salesman had guaranteed results. The materials were expensive and consisted of a variety of workbooks, picture and letter cards for each child, large cards for the teacher to use with the class, and filmstrips and records.

"In the beginning, my kids loved the program," reports Miss Lord. "They thought it was fun to hold up the picture cards that matched the one I was holding and then find the letter that went with the picture and hold that up. Now they groan when I say it's time to get out our picture and letter cards."

"Same thing in my class," agrees Mrs. Washington. "They aren't even too interested in the filmstrips anymore, and the records that go along with the strips can't always be heard. They keep asking me when they're going to get a book."

"Mine want to read from books too; and frankly, I think this program spends far too long on letters and sounds. I'm ready to vote for not using it again next year," comments Mrs. Dorn. "Here it is January and my children aren't as far along as classes I've had in other years.

"I'm ready to scrap it too," Miss Baines says. "The cards are okay, although they weren't worth all that money. I'd use the filmstrips again from time to time—with my commentary —but I don't think we should order those workbooks for next year."

"All right, let's wait till next month's meeting to make a final decision about this, but it seems that we're about ready to give up this Triple L Program. Let's move on to our next topic."

Moral: Beware of salesmen bearing guaranteed results.

Individually Prescribed Instruction

The youngsters in Mr. Carson's fifth grade do most of their subject matter work individually, using a variety of materials available to them. Each pupil works at his own pace on materials prescribed for him, using books, headphones, filmstrips, and so on. This frees Mr. Carson from the presentation of subject matter, and he is supposed to provide help and guidance to his students as they work on content. He moves about the room examining the work of various youngsters.

"Good, Beth." "Donna, that's not what you're supposed to be doing. Pay attention to the instructions." "A little less dreaming, Larry, or you'll never finish your work." "Look how messy that work is, Billy. I'm sure you don't want your papers to look like that." "What's the problem over here? Yes, I see that your answers are wrong, Gloria. You need to check back and see where the problem lies. As usual, you go too fast. . . ."

> **Moral:**   More time allotted for teacher help may not mean more helpful teachers.

Educational Television

"Clear your desks, children," calls Mrs. Melton, "it's time for Spanish."

A few of the third graders comply eagerly and turn to face the television set, but the majority of children grimace and groan.

"Never mind the complaints," rebukes Mrs. Melton, although she too is beginning to be bored with the television language lessons. "It's good to know another language, and we're lucky to have these programs available to us. Now let's pay attention so that we'll hear all the new words."

> **Moral:**   The television message is received in many classrooms with more than medium cool.

Analyzing the Tour

The Findings

What did we find on our tour? Or, perhaps we should begin by asking what we did *not* find. Among other things, we did *not* find teachers asking provocative questions designed to develop thinking skills in their students. Nor did we find youngsters being encouraged to ask questions of teachers or each other; nor were they encouraged to help each other. We did not see adults reacting very warmly to pupils or to other adults. While it is true that our tour was extremely brief, the innovations we observed did not seem to have much effect on the climate of the schools or classrooms we observed or the ways in which teachers behaved.

We *did* find that a team of teachers planned the kind of science lesson so commonly found in one-teacher classrooms, consisting of a teacher demonstration followed by workbook exercises—activities not terribly useful for learning science. We also saw that extending the time youngsters spend in school does not ensure that more learning will take place. If teaching is not effective to begin with, adding to the time spent on subjects may merely add to student disenchantment with learning.

We also found that revising the curriculum, or adding to it, through new math, sex education, Black history, or new reading programs didn't add novel or stimulating behavior. The new reading program was based more on gimmicks than ideas. In the math, history, and sex education classes the teachers' questions asked only for recall on the part of the pupils. The explanation of the math content was confusing and the teacher was so negative as to make many children doubt their adequacy in this subject—a problem many pupils faced in the days of the "old" math.

In general, the effectiveness of television-as-teacher must be questioned when we realize that most youngsters now come to school with five or six years of television viewing behind them yet speak the language of their families and neighborhoods, whether or not it corresponds to that spoken by people they have watched for hundreds of hours on television. Too, a child's cognitive development, in general, is reflective of his home background. Constant bombardment from the TV set doesn't seem to alter that much. What seems vital in learning is the quality of the *interaction* that takes place between the person in the role of teacher and the person who is the learner, and television is pretty much a one-way kind of communication. (Much of the teaching done by humans in our schools is also one-way rather than interactive—teachers send messages, which may or may not be received by pupils.)

Programmed materials that pupils use on an individual basis so that each may progress at his own pace and individually prescribed instruction, which includes programs of varying kinds designed specifically for each pupil, may someday be developed to a high degree of efficiency, but for the most part their content is not now very different from that in standard textbooks— neither provocative nor profound. We would need huge numbers of highly trained persons to prepare materials that are truly individually prescribed for each pupil; and most programmed materials currently flooding the market are poorly conceived and hardly tested in the field. (After all, if the point is to show a profit, why bother with expensive field tests?) The programmed materials are also said to be "teacher-proof," meaning that no teacher can spoil their effect, but there really are no teacher-proof materials, nor should there be unless we plan to do away with human teachers entirely. All teachers affect the materials they use, often unconsciously, so that these materials mesh with their views of teaching and learning. Programmed materials are said to free the teacher to give the kind of helpful guidance to each child which is not possible when so much time must be spent presenting subject matter content; but we saw from our visit to the classroom in which pupils were using individually prescribed programmed materials that that teacher was not able to give effective guidance merely because he was freed from the task of presenting content. That is, additional time did not make him into a helping person.

One school we visited had no grade designations, presumably to permit youngsters to proceed through content at a pace that is logical for them and also to remove the constant judgment and pressure put upon youngsters who are supposed to cover a certain amount of material within a certain time span at a certain age. We saw, however, that a nongraded classroom didn't ensure the removal of the same kinds of pressures placed by teachers on children in other grouping arrangements. Encouraging individual exploration does not depend upon a graded system, since youngsters can merely cover the . same material at different rates in a nongraded system; at the same time, in regular graded classrooms teachers *could* encourage youngsters to move at varying paces, both horizontally and vertically.

Grouping children with those who are akin to them in some dimension like reading ability will not necessarily accomplish intended aims if teaching behavior within these groupings doesn't vary. As we observed, a discouraging teacher can make bright or slow youngsters feel inadequate, and a stimulating curriculum is not an automatic result of new grouping patterns. Neither does the use of paraprofessionals to assist teachers in various ways ensure improved teaching or learning. Differentiated staffing, whether it ultilizes community people, beginning teachers working with senior teachers, or any of the various models for bringing people of varying skills and backgrounds together in teams, will not by itself bring about change, because learning will not be affected merely by adding or subtracting staff or arranging for differing responsibilities according to years of service and amount of preparation.

The Meaning of the Tour

What does all of this mean? Does it mean that none of the innovations we observed should be instituted—that they actually *prevent* effective teaching? Not at all. Our tour was meant to show that certain innovations in and of themselves do not automatically bring about change in the most important area of all, *the quality of human interaction* which occurs in schools and classrooms. Most of the changes seen on our tour could have significant possibilities for education *if* combined with innovations in the ways in which human beings behave with one another.

For example, teams of teachers, or differentiated staffs of varying kinds, *can* provide for the sort of sharing of ideas and feelings among adults which is difficult to achieve under the one-teacher/one-class arrangement. The advantages that could accrue to youngsters who have the chance to work with adults of differing backgrounds, skills, and abilities are self-evident. However, grouping staff together without helping them learn to work well with one another often results in friction among the staff, while not improving the quality of the curriculum or the teaching provided to pupils.

New or revised subjects like sex education or the new mathematics should certainly be incorporated into the curriculum, again for the self-evident reasons that new knowledge or important knowledge ought to be incorporated into our schools. The point of our tour was not that content innovations are worthless but that changing content doesn't necessarily cause changes in the quality of human interaction.

Extending the length of the school day might be an extremely valuable innovation for youngsters whose homes or neighborhoods provide little positive stimulation, or whose parents work or are otherwise unable to provide supervision; but once again the value of this change depends on the quality of the curriculum and the human interaction. Removing the ladder-like quality of so many schools, where all children must climb the grades in exactly the same manner, has obvious advantages, as does grouping pupils with like interests or abilities at certain times for certain activities. However, changing the grouping structure by shuffling youngsters around or changing grade labels doesn't ensure that teaching or learning will change.

Educational television and programmed learning, which often involve computers and other kinds of hardware, clearly have an enormous part to play in our educational future and certainly should be utilized whenever they can provide more than the human beings in the school can offer. Television is useful for bringing to the classroom what cannot be directly experienced; computers can provide information immediately when needed; programs can permit youngsters to move in independent directions or can be used by small groups of youngsters with like needs or interests when their use is more efficient and appropriate than working with peers or adult staff. However, while these things might change the *amount* of human interaction, they will not improve the *quality* of this interaction in schools. These innovations, like the others we have observed, do not *prevent* effective teaching and improved learning, they simply do not ensure its occurrence.

Structure, Content, and Process: Three Categories of Innovation

We have been discussing three kinds of innovation: one involving structure, another concerned with content, and the third having to do with process. All of the innovations observed on our tour can be grouped under the first two areas, those of structure and content. Innovations in structure are those that involve the ways schools and classrooms are organized; for example, time may be added or subtracted from the day or year; personnel can be arranged in a variety of ways; rooms and buildings can be variously arranged. Content innovations are those that introduce subjects not previously dealt with in schools or revise old subject areas in new ways; Black history and the new math are examples of these. The third area, process, has to do with human interaction, and *it is the thesis of this book that the possibilities inherent in any innovation in content or structure cannot be fully realized without accompanying changes in the third area, that of process. Furthermore, it is the thesis of this book that what is currently most needed in our schools is, in fact, process change.*

Process innovation, then, is the subject of this book. We saw on our tour that introducing changes into the areas of content and structure did not change the ways in which human beings behaved toward one another. (One exception is that process is sometimes affected, temporarily, by newness; that is, teachers may become enthusiastic about a new program and transmit this enthusiasm and interest to pupils, who then learn more because of an improved learning climate. However, when the newness and the enthusiasm are gone, the effect is gone.)

What are some process innovations involving human behavior that would benefit our schools? One would be changing the questioning patterns of teachers by teaching them to ask questions calling for imagination and thought on the part of the pupils rather than mere recall and retrieval. Questions asked according to a kind of logic that would build pupils' thinking in a sequential manner would be another desirable process change. Still other changes would affect the entire pattern of pupil and teacher talk in a number of ways: expanding the amount of pupil talk, increasing the amount of pupil-to-pupil talk, acknowledging and dealing with the existence of feelings, decreasing the amount of controlling and censorious talk on the part of teachers, and so on.

Other worthy process changes could occur around the important area of decision-making, with teachers encouraging pupils to share in making vital decisions which bear upon their daily learning lives; administrators sharing decision-making power with teachers and other school personnel; and the staff working more effectively with parents. This would be a departure from the usual procedure, which is to have the person with the most powerful position act as the almost unquestioned arbiter in all matters. (American schools all too often have a thin veneer of token democracy, covering a truly repressive and controlling environment. The veneer consists of such tokenisms as classroom officers elected by their peers but with no influence on policy; talk *about* democracy but little in the way of example or practice; pupils being permitted to decide about such matters as which person will follow them in leading a game or which of five countries they would like to report on to the class; teachers deciding whether they want to order the reading series of publisher X or publisher Y.)

Still other process innovations that could improve the ways in which people behave with one another would be the encouragement of cooperation rather than competition; success *with* others rather than at the expense of others; the establishment of a climate that encourages pupils to say "I need help," without being made to feel stupid and that permits teachers to say the same without worrying about jeopardizing their careers; the establishment of a spirit among school personnel that inspires them to work together to improve learning conditions for children.

Process involves the cognitive, or intellectual, domain as well as the affective, or social and emotional, realm of education. The ensuing chapters will suggest specific ways in which teachers and prospective teachers, youngsters, and all others who are or will be in schools can encounter one another in more expansive, productive, and satisfying ways.

2 encounter: learning about ourselves and others

This chapter will present a number of activities[1] designed to help you encounter yourselves and others more honestly and openly, so that you may know more about, care more about, and live more fully with yourselves and others. The focus will be personal and interpersonal, and the objective is to make you

[1] The activities described in this chapter are known to me primarily because of my work with the NTL Institute for Applied Behavioral Science. It is impossible to give credit to the originators of many of these ideas, because there is so much sharing of ideas, and also modifying and adapting ideas, among persons associated with NTL. Because of this, and

aware of some of your own and other people's feelings. Reading about the procedures in advance will not detract from participation; in fact, you can go through many of the exercises a number of times and experience new learning each time.

A classroom exercise, some resulting discussion, and some comments upon the resultant learnings will be presented in detail first, to be followed by a number of other activities for use in your own setting.

Who Will Volunteer?

Nearly every semester some incident occurs in my classes which indicates that many students are reluctant to volunteer if this means leading the class in some way, even if volunteering only means being more visible than the other class members. When this happens, I introduce an activity designed to help people confront their feelings about putting themselves up for a leading role in class; in addition, this method makes it possible to learn how others feel about volunteering.

I begin the exercise by saying, "We're going to need a few volunteers today to lead us in an activity. Who is willing to volunteer?" After giving the class a few moments to consider whether or not they will volunteer, I tell them that this time we are not actually going to have volunteers but instead will *all* participate in an exercise which will help us look at our feelings about volunteering. "Let's all close our eyes, and then, when you are settled comfortably, each of you have a conversation inside your head between the you who wants to volunteer and the you who doesn't. Just let yourself go and actually have these two talk to each other, each one trying to convince the other. Continue the conversation until one or the other wins, and really try to stay with it until I ask you to open your eyes."

After two or three minutes I say, "All right, let's open our eyes for a moment while listening to the next instructions. This

because collaboration is the very nature of the NTL Institute for Applied Behavioral Science, I would like to credit NTL in general, and all those interns, network members, and participants with whom I have worked.

time you will bring your antagonists back together and have them encounter each other without words. While they won't talk to each other, they will use some nonverbal means to try to win out. Close your eyes now, and if possible stay with this until one or the other prevails."

After another minute or so for this part of the procedure, we open our eyes and I ask those who are willing to share experiences with the rest of us. If the group is very large or the time relatively short, the class does this in groups of five or six, taking some time for total class sharing. Otherwise we do the entire activity as a total class. Even though I have gone through this exercise many times, I am always surprised at how many students are hesitant about volunteering—students whose timid or "underdog" self prevails.

A typical classroom conversation after the fantasy has been completed might sound like this. "Well, my volunteer self won out, but my nonvolunteer self kept saying, 'You're just showing off and being pushy.' When the two came together without words, my volunteer self socked my other self on the jaw!"

"I decided not to volunteer because my nonvolunteer self kept saying that the class would see how stupid I was, and since there were so many others who can do things well, why should I make a fool of myself? When we did the nonverbal stuff, they just sort of pushed each other around."

"My nonvolunteer self won also, not because he said I was stupid but because he insisted that others could do it better. And he's right!"

"Well, my person who said not to volunteer pointed out that people might laugh if I made mistakes, so it was better not to try anything. If I just stayed quietly in my seat no one would know, and no one would laugh. When they came together afterward, the volunteer self put her arm around the nonvolunteer self—to comfort her, I guess."

"I decided to volunteer rather easily, but I had some of the same feelings that someone else mentioned. My nonvolunteer self kept saying that other people would think I was presumptuous and just trying to hog the spotlight. When they fought it out without words, my volunteer self just smashed the other one with a big board."

"I also felt that others would resent me if I volunteered. But my volunteer self won out anyway."

"I was afraid to volunteer, but he (the volunteer) won out because he said, 'I don't care what you say, *coward*, I'm going to do it.' Then the nonvolunteer chased the volunteer, but he got away. It was sort of a 'to hell with you, I'm going to do this no matter what you say' kind of thing."

This sharing of fantasies leads to a realization of how widespread feelings of inadequacy are among class members, and also results, for many, in a sense of relief at the discovery that they are not alone in their timidity. There is also some recognition that fears of not doing well, or even of provoking laughter from classmates, may result logically from past experience but may no longer be appropriate. And there is usually reassurance for each other about group support; that laughing at each other or putting each other down will not happen. There is also the discovery that many persons who seem to participate easily worry about how they are being received. Each class member must decide for himself how he will deal with what has happened, but the main learning, I believe, comes from the sharing of feelings of concern in an atmosphere which encourages openness and trust.

Either toward the end of this class session or at some time soon after, I ask what the learning from this activity means to teachers and future teachers. We talk about what teachers can do to help children feel comfortable about volunteering and speculate that if feelings of inadequacy are present in persons who have had successful school careers, these feelings may be quite severe in persons who experience either failure or only occasional success in their school lives. I have found this exercise, "Who Will Volunteer," to be an extremely effective one, and I can recommend its use with children as well as adults.

Sharing and Caring

When we care about others and trust them to care about us, we will be more at ease with ourselves and others, less hostile and more affectionate, less constrained and more open; we will feel less put upon, used, or wronged, and we will be more careful about using others like objects. We will, in other words, be more human. Feelings of affection and acceptance are nurtured in an atmosphere of openness and caring; teachers and administrators can help build this kind of atmosphere in classrooms and schools, or they can stifle feelings of trust and encourage feelings of constraint and hostility by creating environments which are mildly or severely oppressive.

Most people want to live in a warm, caring atmosphere and provide such an environment for others, and one way to achieve this is to share thoughts and feelings with others in an encouraging and accepting milieu. The activities in this chapter are presented to provide teachers and future teachers with some means for building sharing and caring environments for themselves and their students and for themselves and their co-workers. It is important to know that the activities are *not* designed to bring tranquillity to difficult situations by encouraging people to "cool it"; rather, they are meant to serve as energizers which will help people care enough about themselves and others to bring about needed change.

All of the following activities may be led by any intelligent and sensitive person—the course instructor or student members of the class, if this is a college or university classroom; any individual member of a school staff, if the exercises are to be used in school faculty meetings or workshops; most probably by a teacher, if they are used in elementary or secondary school classrooms.

Microlabs*

Laboratory learning is a term used to describe the process of learning about yourself and others, and the groups and organizations to which you belong, through the direct experience of participating in groups specifically formed for this purpose.

---

* I want to thank Dr. William C. Schutz for introducing me to microlabs, to many of the activities included in this chapter, and, in fact, to the whole field of encounter.

A *microlab* is a planned selection of activities derived from the many possibilities inherent in laboratory learning—a sampling of what might occur in labs or groups—such as sensitivity training groups, encounter groups, T (for training) groups, or human relations groups.

The microlabs presented here are planned for small groups of from three to six persons; if the groups are larger, it is difficult for everyone to have a chance to share. All groups should be about the same size, so that each group will have an equal amount of time to go through each activity. Otherwise, if there is one group of six people and one group of four, the group of four will probably be finished with each assignment long before the larger group. The activities included are meant to help bring people closer together.

When going through these microlabs, try to keep the "judgmental you" in abeyance. In other words, try to let yourself go with the activities without judging their worth at the time and without thinking about what you will tell this or that friend afterwards. Try to stay with the suggested topics rather than moving off into the more usual kinds of chitchat, and try to be open and honest. Refrain from giving advice to others—just listen, discover, and share. Try to remember to look at the persons to whom you are speaking, and say, "*You* seem to me to be . . ." rather than "*He* seems" or "*John* seems." Make an effort to say "I" when speaking of yourself, that is, "*I* feel hurt when that happens" rather than, "You know how you feel hurt when that happens." This will help you to "own" your own feelings. If your small group does not have time for everyone to have a turn on any given part, those who did not have a chance to participate on the previous task might start the new round.

Forming Microlab Groups

There are a number of ways to form microlab groups, and you can select those that seem most appropriate to your situation. You can, of course, just count off and form random groups. You can form microlab groups according to natural work groups, especially if you want this experience to carry over for future use. In a college classroom this might mean that those who teach or plan to teach a certain age group or subject, and may work together on future projects, should arrange to be with those whose interests are similar. People can select each other according to any logical dimension, for example, those they have thus far had little opportunity to know, those they would *like* to know better, or those seen as different from themselves according to race, age, sex, or outlook.

When groups are being formed according to interest, or with people who work together, then these persons can merely get together after it has been determined who they are. If there are too many persons for one group, they can split accordingly. If other dimensions are being used, it may be that a number of persons representing the total number of groups to be formed (six persons for six groups) will be selected, and they will then select others for their groups. They can each select one other person, with these two deciding upon a third person, these three on a fourth, and so on. This can be done with or without words. When forming groups nonverbally, the first person usually goes up to the person with whom he wants to work and takes his hand; then these two take the hand of a third, and this goes on until the group is completed.

One person should be designated in advance to give the instructions to the others, and he may or may not participate in the microlab. If he does become a member of a group, he will need to keep an eye on other groups so he can be aware of when to move on to the next activity. Every group may not finish every assignment, but each should be encouraged to move on to the next part of the microlab whether or not all members have had a turn. Time periods are listed after each activity, but these are meant to be used as guides, not as absolutes.

Microlab I (approximate time 40–50 minutes)

Remember! Try to:
    Avoid being judgmental.
    Stay with suggested topics.
    Listen and discover, rather than give advice.

Be open and honest.
Look at people when you speak to them.
Say "I" when speaking of yourself.
Say "you" when speaking to another.
If anyone has been left out of any round because of lack
of time, start the new round with that person.

1. Form small groups of from three to six persons, according to instructions given on page 24. Seat yourselves close together in a circle, leaving as much space as possible between the different circles. (three minutes)
2. Share first impressions of each other; these may include negative as well as positive feelings. (four minutes)
3. Tell each other the *one* thing you would most like the other members of your group to know about you. Whatever pops into your head is appropriate. (four minutes)
4. Share something about yourself which you would not ordinarily tell the others. Here there will be a tendency to censor, but try not to censor too far down your list before you share something. (four minutes)
5. Tell the other members of your group about a vivid elementary school memory. Again, whatever pops into your head will be relevant. (five minutes)
6. Make yourself very small in fantasy, and enter your own body. Travel around inside yourself for several minutes. (two minutes) Then share with each other what you saw. (four minutes)
7. What have been your strongest feelings (anger, joy, sadness, hatred, for example) in the past two or three days, and what caused these feelings? (five minutes)
8. Once again, share impressions of each other. (five minutes)

9. Give each other a gift, something that will probably be nonmaterial, like a quality. If time is limited, each person can give a gift only to the person to his right or to his right and left. (five minutes)

The gift giving is the last activity of this first microlab. When the activity has ended, the total group may want to spend time talking about their experiences. However, this is not essential; each person can take away his own experience and his own meaning without any total group discussion.

Microlab II (approximate time 45–55 minutes)

1. Begin with the same people you worked with for microlab I, and include newcomers into groups in any convenient way. Arrange yourselves once again into closely knit circles, as far away as possible from other groups.
   a. Settle yourselves comfortably in your chairs. Close your eyes and relax. Just get with yourself—sense yourself. (two minutes)
   b. Notice the part of your body you are most aware of. Concentrate on that part and try to let all of your feeling move to that part of your body. (one minute)
   c. Now try consciously to move your awareness into some other part of your body that you are not now aware of and concentrate on that. Try to let all your feeling move to that part of your body. (one minute)
   d. Become aware of the tips of your fingers (thirty seconds), your toes (thirty seconds), the tip of your nose (thirty seconds).
   e. With eyes still closed, put the palms of your hands on your upper chest and become aware of your breathing. (one minute) Move your hands to your abdomen and feel your breathing there. (one min-

ute) Sense the air as it enters and leaves your nostrils. (one minute)

f. Take your face in your hands and explore your face and neck in a gentle and caring manner. (one minute)

g. Embrace yourself, with your hands on your upper arms. Just hold yourself for awhile. Tell yourself something good about yourself. (one minute)

h. Now just get with yourself again, and sense yourself as a person inside your own skin, separate from all others. (one minute)

i. With your eyes still closed, join hands with the other members of your group. (one minute) Now open your eyes, drop hands slowly, and look into the eyes of each member of your group.

2. Talk about your feelings now. Remember to say *"I feel,"* and look at others as you speak. (four minutes)

3. Tell each other about your very first memory. (five minutes)

4. Tell each other which part of your body you like least; which most. (four minutes)

5. Arrange to have two members of your group move to another group. That means that if there are five persons in your group, two will leave for another group and two from another group will join you. The two who move should stay together, and each group should decide together which two members will leave. (three minutes)

6. When the new groups are formed, tell each other how you usually feel when you enter a new group. (four minutes)

7. Share with each other the best thing that ever happened to you. (four minutes)

8. Share with each other the worst, or saddest, thing that ever happened to you. (five minutes)

9. Tell each other of a vivid secondary school memory. (five minutes)

10. Close your eyes for a moment and give a gift to yourself—probably something nonmaterial. (forty seconds) Now tell the others what it was. (three minutes)

11. Close your eyes again, get comfortable, and just get with yourself. (one minute) Take the hands of your fellow group members and slowly open your eyes. Say goodbye to each group member with your eyes, without words, and then drop hands.

Microlab III (approximate time 40–50 minutes)

In this last programmed microlab, you might arrange for new small groups by getting with as many new people as possible, especially if one goal is to get to know other people in the total group; you might return to your original group, if your goal is to get to know one specific group as well as possible; or you can vary group membership in any way you like.

1. Talk with each other, with no set agenda, for ten minutes. Try to avoid "cocktail party chatter," express your feelings, and continue to be open and honest with one another. (ten minutes)

2. Complete the following sentences, using paper and pencil:
   a. Sometimes I think I'm _____.
   b. People don't like me when I _____.
   c. People like me when I _____.
   d. I feel hurt when _____.
   e. I feel happy when _____.
   f. The thing about me that I'd like to change is _____.
   g. The best thing about me is _____.
   h. I really am _____.
   Share the results with each other. (twelve minutes)

3. What are some problems you have in your life now? (seven minutes)
4. What are some satisfactions you have in your life now? (seven minutes)
5. Pretend that you have only twenty-four hours left to live. Think silently for a few moments about how you would spend this time. (two minutes) Share your thoughts with the others. (five minutes)
6. Stand and form a circle with your small group. Take turns having each member stand in the center of the circle, with eyes closed, while the other group members show him one at a time and without words how they feel about him. These feelings may be positive or negative and will have to be shown through touching. When everyone has had a turn, sit down and talk about what happened. (five minutes)
7. Get comfortable in your seats, close your eyes, and get with yourself. Sense yourself. (two minutes) Embrace yourself and silently tell yourself something good about yourself. (one minute) With eyes still closed, join with the other members of your group. (one minute) Open eyes, drop hands slowly, and say goodbye to each fellow group member in a way which is in keeping with the spirit of our three microlabs.

As always, you may want to have some total group discussion about this experience, or you may not—what you do is up to you and your group.

A Microlab for Youngsters

1. Have the children get into small groups of three or four. These groups may be set up by the teacher in advance, or children may select each other on any of the dimensions listed for adult microlabs. Or have only one group meet at a time, with you, in which

case the groups might be larger. It is very important to refrain from criticizing the pupils for what they say, and you should probably join in as a member. The rest of the class can observe or be doing other work.

2. Tell each other what you dislike most about school.
3. Share with each other something you *do* like about school.
4. Pretend you are going to become teachers, and tell something you remember from school life that would help you be a better teacher.
5. Tell about the best thing that ever happened to you outside of school.
6. Tell about the worst or saddest thing that ever happened to you outside of school.
7. Tell something that you don't like about yourself.
8. Tell something that you *do* like about yourself.
9. Complete the following sentences: (may be done orally)
   a. When I am scolded I _____.
   b. I worry about _____.
   c. I feel happy when _____.
   d. I get mad when _____.
10. If you could change one thing in your life, what would it be?
11. What are some reasons you like people?
12. What are some things about *you* which people like?
13. What could this class, including the teacher, do to help you?

Additional Microlab Possibilities

The following list of other possibilities for small group activities can be used for more microlabs in your undergraduate or graduate classes, in your schools with co-workers, or with youngsters. You will have to be the judge of which ones to use, and of when and how and with whom to use them. They are listed here in no particular sequence.

1. For very young children you might want to include activities that do not require words. For example, go and pick someone you like and show him that you like him; pick someone you don't like and make an angry face at him; show us with your body that you are happy, or sad; show us how you could make someone who is sad feel better.

2. Sentence completions of various kinds:
   a. I'd like to tell my teacher that _____.
   b. If I could be someone else, I'd be _____.
   c. When I come into the school building, I feel

      _____.

   d. When I talk in front of the class I feel

      _____.

   e. If I could change one thing in this school it would be _____.
   f. When I lose an argument or a game I feel

      _____.

   g. I feel happy (sad, angry, proud, shy, upset, and so on) when _____.
   h. When it's time for math (or any other subject) I

      _____.

   i. When I'm alone I _____.
   j. If I were a teacher, I'd _____.
   k. I feel like yelling (smiling, crying, hitting, and so on) when _____.

3. What would you most like to happen to you as a result of this course (this school year, these meetings)?

4. What will your life be like five years from today? This may be told as you really think it will be or as you wish it to be.

5. Tell about your favorite teacher and your least favor-

ite teacher, using as data all the teachers you've ever had.

6. Share your dream of glory with the group.

7. Pick a new name for yourself, consulting with the group on your choice.

8. Decide what makes of cars the different members of the group remind you of. Food, colors, animals, houses, and so on, can also be used in this analogy game.

9. What gift would you like to give to a child in your class with whom you have difficulty. (for teachers)

10. What gift would you like to give to yourself in your role as parent, teacher, student, or child.

11. Fantasize about the others in your group as children —or as old people.

12. The money game: Everyone will bring money to the group, without telling others how much he plans to bring, and each will put out in front of him whatever amount he has brought. The group will discuss the varying amounts. Then each person will put whatever money he is willing to part with into a pool in the center, keeping the rest in front of him. Then everyone takes money from the pool according to what he wants to take, and each may continue to take as long as there is any money there. At the end, feelings about giving and taking money and what it means to each person will be discussed.

13. Paper images: Have a large supply of paper of various textures and colors, plus scissors, scotch tape, clips, and glue. First, ask each person to select a piece of paper of the color he thinks best represents him. Everyone places this in front of himself, and other group members merely note what has been chosen. Then, everyone makes an image of himself in paper— not a realistic figure but a representation—using as

many colors, textures, and shapes as needed. When all are finished, each person keeps his image in front of himself, and he and the group discuss what they see and what was meant. (An additional activity, at the end of the discussion, can consist of staking out some floor space [the center of the circle, for example] and asking each member to place his image on the floor space according to some dimension, with the center of the circle being the focal point. Group members might place their images according to how influential they think they are in the group, how active they are, how easy they are to confront, how helpful, and so on.)

14. Action sociograms: People can line themselves up, or place themselves in chairs which have been previously lined up, with one end of the line being "most" and the other end being "least," according to dimensions of influence, aggression, and so on. Some possible topics for lining up in action sociograms, in addition to those mentioned under "paper images" are: how cooperative I am, how well I handle my anger, how good I feel about myself. Group members can be permitted to move other members if they believe those others are in the wrong spot, and if a person is moved to the same spot by two different persons, he must stay there. (A variation of the action sociogram is to have *one* group member line all the others up according to one of these dimensions.) The discussion following the activity will be most important.

15. Secrets: Each person writes a secret he has, anonymously, on a piece of paper. All papers are placed in a pile, and everyone draws one out, reads it aloud, and then tells how he thinks it might feel to have this particular secret. Secrets may be "owned" or not, depending on personal wishes.

16. The paper bag self: Everyone is given a paper bag,

and there are picture magazines, glue, magic markers, scissors, scotch tape, and colored paper available to the total group. On the outside of the paper bag, each person puts what he wants other people to know about him, and what he thinks is obvious about him. Inside he puts what he thinks others don't know about him, and what he doesn't want them to know. In the sharing time, people discuss their bags, sharing only what they care to about their inner bag "selves."

The activities in this chapter were included, as stated earlier, to help in the creation of more open and caring environments. In addition, they were designed to help you and your pupils focus upon personal and interpersonal feelings and recognize the important part that feelings play in all of our lives. The next chapter, indeed, the rest of this book, will continue to deal with feelings, with behavior, and with change.

Selected References

George Brown. *Human Teaching for Human Learning,* The Viking Press, Inc., New York, 1971.

Bernard Gunther. *Sense Relaxation,* P. F. Collier, Inc., New York, 1968.

The Journal of Applied Behavior Science, NTL Institute for Applied Behavioral Science, 1201 Sixteenth Street, N.W., Washington, D.C. 20036.

J. William Pfeiffer and John E. Jones. *A Handbook of Structured Experiences for Human Relations Training,* Vol. I, II, and III, University Associates Press, P.O. Box 615, Iowa City, Iowa 52240, 1969, 1970, 1971.

10 Exercises for Trainers, NTL Institute for Applied Behavioral Science, 1201 Sixteenth Street, N.W., Washington, D.C. 20036.

William C. Schutz. *Joy: Expanding Human Awareness,* Grove Press, Inc., New York, 1967.

3

change:
working toward
more effective behavior

The episodes and activities in this chapter are included so that
you may become more skilled in observing and analyzing your
own and other people's behavior in groups. You will, of course,
adopt only the behaviors you want to adopt; however, you must
"try on" new behaviors before you can decide which ones you
would like to own. Before we engage in any "trying on" exer-
cizes, let us look at three examples of group behavior by visiting
three faculty meetings. All three staffs deal with the same topic,
but the behavior evidenced will be quite different.

A Faculty Meeting in School X

Scene I: The Conference Room

"I've just found out," says Mr. Grissom, the principal, beginning the meeting, "that we've been selected as one of the schools to be included in the experimental individualized learning programs for next year. Now, we've got quite a bit of work to do in this whole field if we're to be ready by next year. We'll have to order many materials, we'll have to look at ways of keeping records of children's progress, and we'll probably want to talk with some experts who are already familiar with this system. We have fairly good equipment in the school, but, as you know, this program means that each teacher will need, just as one example, a couple of hundred books kept right in the classroom—so we have a lot of work to do. I'm very pleased about our selection as one of the pilot schools for this project, and I'm sure we're all going to work hard to make the program a success. Now, I'd like you, Mary, to be in charge of the committee to look into the ordering of materials, and I thought that Jack, Mrs. Lindgren, and Miss Foley could complete that committee. In addition, we need a committee to look at what's been done in this field, and perhaps invite some people in to talk with us. Bill, would you be in charge of that committee, and, let's see, who would like to volunteer to work with Bill on this? We just need two or three others. Can I see some hands? It won't be a great deal of work, but it will be an important assignment. All right, thank you, Mrs. Jonas. Anyone else? Thank you, Peggy." There was another pause, and then Mr. Grissom said, "Well, I guess two will be enough. Now, to move on to our next item of business. . . ."

Scene II: The Faculty Room

"Well, Bill, don't you feel honored to be in charge of that important committee?" asked Joe Long, sarcastically. "It's such a big job I don't know if you'll be able to handle it. However, you're lucky to have Mr. Grissom around to help you along. In fact, now that I think of it, you probably won't have to do much, because Mr. Grissom will undoubtedly have quite a few ideas all set to share with you."

"That Grissom absolutely infuriates me with his phony pretenses. I mean, he is really out of the dark ages! He doesn't even ask us what *we* want to do about this new program," complained Jean Ventura. "He picks people for committees without consulting us, and then throws in a pretense at some kind of democracy by asking for volunteers! Did you notice how eager everyone was to volunteer? It's a good thing we only have staff meetings once a month, because if we had them more often I think I'd explode!"

"Don't get so excited, Jean," said Don Koler. "Do what I do, which is to attend in body only. I learned long ago to sit toward the back and bring something to do—even if it's only a crossword puzzle. Old Grissom is going to get up there and sound off about things he could have sent us notices about, and that's that. So—it's two hours a month wasted. Don't let it get you."

"What annoys me," said Barbara Feldman, "is that we're going to be involved in a new program next year, and we were never even consulted about it. I approve of individualized learning programs, and it will be great to have some good new materials, but frankly, Grissom turns me off so much I don't even feel like participating."

"Well, I don't approve of individualized learning programs, at least not for many of my children," Miles Ford joined in. "Many of the youngsters in my classes need much more structure than they'll find in this individualized fad. It's okay for some, mind you, but not all."

"What's all the fuss about? We all do what we want anyway, when the doors are closed," said Joe Long. "I'll have my class running the way I want, just as I always do, and so will all the rest of you."

"Right! This new program will end up the same as all the rest of Grissom's schemes," agreed Don Koler. "Now, let's go home—we've been here since eight o'clock this morning. Anyone want a ride downtown?"

A Faculty Meeting in School Y

Scene I: The Conference Room

"I've just found out," announced Mr. Middleton, the principal, "that we've been selected as one of the schools which will be using individualized learning programs next year. Now, we've got quite a bit of work to do if we are to be ready by next September. We'll need a materials committee, and a committee to . . ."

"Wait a minute, wait a minute!" Lew Block interrupted. "I'd like a little history on this, and I'd like to know why we weren't asked before this whether or not we wanted to be in the program, and I'd also like to know a lot more about the whole idea."

"The history, of this, Mr. Block," said Mr. Middleton coldly, "is that the assistant superintendent in charge of new programs looked around at schools which were considered good enough to put into effect some new and interesting programs, and ours was chosen. I consider it an honor, but you evidently don't."

"Maybe it is an honor and maybe it isn't, but what I want to know is why we're never consulted about anything. Surely you've heard of participatory democracy," Mr. Block smiled sarcastically. "I believe that just last week you sent around a memo saying that it was important for us to involve our pupils in planning and so on."

"We've always gotten along so well in the past," said Mrs. Blandinger rather nervously. "I don't see what the argument is about. Now I think it's just grand that we've been chosen, and I think it's lovely that we're going to have a chance to do something new and interesting."

"Sure, you always got along well in the past. You never

questioned any decisions from above, and you always do what you're told. Why shouldn't you get along!"

"Well, if you're through, Mr. Block, I'll go on with what I was saying. We need a number of committees to get things going, and I'd like Jeff Wright to chair the materials committee and Vera Pearson to chair the committee which we might call research and development—to fill us in on the latest developments in this field."

"Mr. Middleton, I must challenge your right to *appoint* people as chairman of committees," said Mr. Block.

"I have to back Lew on that, Mr. Middleton," said Kathy O'Neill. "It doesn't seem right for all these decisions to be made by one person."

"I wish," said Quentin Rider, "that people would stop interrupting. We'll be here all night at this rate. Let's just hear about the program!"

"Mr. Rider is quite right," said Mrs. Greer. "If we can't even listen to Mr. Middleton with respect, how do we expect our youngsters to listen to us, I'd like to know."

"I don't expect my pupils to listen to me with respect unless I have something worth listening to," said Mr. Block, "but I suppose that's something you wouldn't understand. You know, Mrs. Greer, 'the times, they are a-changing.' This is a new world, with new ideas and new kids; but you'd never know it around here!"

"Thank goodness none of our pupils come to our staff meetings," said Myrtle Everson. "Can you imagine what they'd think of us if they could see us arguing this way?"

"Maybe it would be good for them," said Kathy. "But anyway, it doesn't seem to me that this program is being instituted in a fair way. I happen to think the *idea* is good, but I don't like the procedure."

"Well, what difference does the procedure make? I don't feel like being on eight million committees to decide what kinds of programs we're going to have in this school. I have enough work to do now. So let's get going and see what we have to do to get it started," said Agnes Polk.

"Come on, let's get going." "What good is all this?" accompanied by groans and annoyed looks came from various people for various reasons, and Mr. Middleton said, "Well, it's unfortunate that we've had this disruption again from a few people. Certainly everyone here has a voice, but it does seem to me that there are constructive and destructive ways of being heard. Now let me see, just from a show of hands, how many want this program to go into effect. That's almost everyone here, as you can see, Mr. Block. So let's get on with it. Anyone who wants to work with Jeff Wright or Vera Pearson can let them know and join the committee. Is that democratic enough for you, Mr. Block?"

Scene II: The Faculty Room

"Listen, just what do you think you're going to accomplish, Block?" asked Quentin Rider. "In case you don't know, I'll tell you. You won't be here next year, because you don't have tenure, and Mr. Middleton will get rid of you. In the meantime, you're just making things uncomfortable for the rest of us. And you're wasting our time at meetings. This is a fine school with a good reputation, and we don't need any advice from newcomers who don't know anything about us. If you're such a flaming do-gooder, go to some school where they can use you."

"*You* may think this is a good school, but *I* can't agree with you. The kids are well behaved, it's true, but a good school is a bit more than that."

"Mr. Block," said Mrs. Greer, "I've been in this school for twenty years, and we never had any quarrels with each other till you came here. Now I'm not saying that we didn't have our disagreements, but we handled them like civilized people. We didn't argue just for the sake of arguing, and we knew how to show respect for leadership. Being chosen to participate in this new program happens to be an honor for our school, but you don't seem to understand that!"

"I understand plenty! It's you people who don't understand

too much! You're just a bunch of sheep who let anybody who happens to be in a higher position than you lead you around. Well, I'm not a sheep, strange as that may seem to you. Oh, what's the use!" and Lew Block left in a rage.

Faculty Meeting in School Z

"I've just found out," said Mr. Fareweather, "that we've been selected as one of the schools which will be using individualized learning programs next year. Now this is considered by the board to be an honor, but I want to know what you people feel about the program."

"Well, for one thing, we have clearly said that from now on our staff would have to take part in initiating any new programs instituted in our school, and this program would violate our stand," said Ron Washington.

"On the other hand, it would be silly to turn something down that was good, just because we didn't have a hand in its initiation," Mr. Fareweather spoke again.

"Let's all put our cards out on the table," suggested Linda Greenspan. "If you have some hidden agenda to get us to accept this program, Mr. Fareweather, I'd feel better if you'd just bring it out into the open."

"You're right, Jane—thanks for calling that to my attention. I should say right from the start that I *would* like us to be in on this plan. It means certain benefits for us—very tangible things like over a thousand new library books, and a great deal of other equipment. And, of course, it is an honor to be chosen, no matter what we may think of the method. However, I want to say that I'll certainly abide by whatever decision we make, and I don't want to sway people through my position as principal—though I hope I may sway them by my arguments!"

"Well, I still feel hesitant about disagreeing with you, Mr. Fareweather," said Theresa Rocco, "but I'm determined, after our human relations training sessions, to be more outspoken. So I'd like to say that if we are ever going to get the central office to include us in on things, we have to take some drastic stands. Now, we're a desirable school, so they want us, and they'll really sit up and take notice if we turn them down."

"I think we should turn them down too, and I think we should send a notice to all the other schools in the district saying why we have done so," said Ron Washington.

"Well, wait a minute, there's such a thing as cutting off our nose to spite our face," Don Cheever, the librarian, said. "I don't think I'd ever forgive any of you if you turned down all those books. Think what they'll mean to our kids!"

"But that's the way we get co-opted by the system every time. We'll go along with things once again, because of the goodies we get," came from Mary Kahn.

"Why can't we accept, and write a letter to the appropriate people saying what we've just been saying, telling why we accepted and why we think it's important that from now on we be consulted—and making it very clear that after this we won't be a part of any program we haven't had a hand in from the outset," suggested Alice King.

"I'm not so sure we should write anything to anyone. Are we going to put individual names on it or what? And will Mr. Fareweather sign?" asked Vera Weeks.

"Oh, for heavens sake, there's that mouse behavior again, and I thought you were going to change that. Who cares if Mr. Fareweather signs or not! What matters is being willing to stand up for what you believe in," said Ron Washington.

"And there's that same impatient and critical behavior from you, Ron," said Jane Greenspan.

"Okay, okay. I'm going to try again, because I do want to change that. Well, I don't know what to say. When you do that, Vera, you make me mad."

"How about saying nothing, then. I can say, Vera, that I understand that you feel worried about our standing up to the central office, and I sympathize with you. However, if we think something is important, then we need to take action, even if we do feel somewhat worried about it," said Jane.

"Well, I know I shouldn't be a mouse, and that's what I said I was going to work on after our training sessions. I do feel worried about writing, though, and when you attack me, Ron, I feel more worried than ever, and resentful, besides. Jane, your statement was helpful."

"Selma, you look as if you've been wanting to say something," said Mr. Fareweather.

"Well, it seems to me that it would be a mistake to turn down a program which would obviously benefit our children. I can't conceive of saying no, and I'd feel really rotten if we turned it down."

"I understand how you feel, Selma," said Mary, "but sometimes principles are more important than a bunch of materials."

"Listen, do we want this stuff or not?" asked Manley Barker. "What's all this fiddling around with feelings? It just wastes time, and we aren't getting anywhere."

"Well, most of us don't feel that this is a waste of time, and we believe—or, I guess I can only speak for myself—*I* believe that our staff meetings have improved tremendously since we've learned to speak more openly with each other and to explore our feelings and opinions before we take action," said Theresa.

"Well, we seem to agree that the program itself is worthwhile," Mr. Fareweather began to summarize, "at least I haven't heard anyone speak against individualized learning programs. Is there anyone who thinks the idea itself is without value? All right, then, we're speaking only about whether to participate or not, and we've heard a number of points of view—that we should go along this time; that we go along but write a letter stating our objections to the way in which the program was initiated; that we go along and write a letter of objection to the method, and say that from now on we expect to be included in plans; that we don't accept and state our reasons to the proper authorities. Have I left anything out?"

"That we write our objections to the other schools in the district," added Ron.

"I'd like to speak for accepting the plan and writing a diplomatic note saying that we are accepting, but that in the future we would like to be included in such plans from their inception. I think we should actually suggest some machinery for having school representatives in on all planning that emanates from the superintendent's office," said Jane.

"Okay. And how about taking the initiative of inviting a representative from the superintendent's office to meet with us at our next staff meeting to discuss this, and begin setting up procedures to be followed in the future," added Ken Heller.

"That sounds good to me, too. And I'd like to suggest that our note be signed by the entire staff. Either everyone's name or everyone except Mr. Fareweather. However, I think it would be important for your name to be included," Ron said to the principal.

"I'm willing to go along with that," responded Mr. Fareweather.

"Well, I'm still not so sure we should say yes," said Mary Kahn, "but I'll go along with it. It would have been quite a jolt to the central office to be turned down, and I think it would have been good for them."

"I'm still tempted to turn them down too, Mary," Ron said, "but I guess I'm willing to give the central office a chance to set up some procedures for including us in the future. If that doesn't work, then we can think about ways to jolt them—and believe me, you and I can come up with plenty of possibilities!"

"Well, I hear pretty wide agreement that we accept the program and make known our desire to be included in all future planning. Is that where we are?" asked Mr. Fareweather, looking around. "That seems to be the final decision. Let's move on to our next item of business."

Some Comments on the XYZ Faculty Meetings

The behavior of participants in the three staff meetings differed rather markedly. In the first school, only the principal spoke at the meeting itself, and there was no audible disagreement, at the time, with what he had to say, but it was quite clear from the conversation afterwards in the faculty room that there were feelings of dissatisfaction with the plan, with the principal's behavior, and with school faculty meetings in general. Some of the teachers made it clear that they planned to sabotage the program, each in his own way. Such behavior is not unusual when people have no say in what is expected of them or do not agree with the plan they are expected to carry out. Disagreement in school X was not overt at the meeting, but was evidenced later in behind-the-scenes griping. It seems unlikely that any remedial action, beyond griping, will be undertaken by the faculty of school X.

In school Y we saw some disagreement during the meeting itself, expressed in hostile and attacking ways, and we saw at least one attempt to deny the controversy. In general, feelings and opinions were expressed unproductively, and in the faculty room afterwards the bickering continued, and arguments remained as unresolved as in the meeting itself.

School Z had several factors in its favor, one, the entire staff had recently had some training sessions to learn to work more collaboratively with each other; another, the principal believed in cooperative planning. Wide and varied participation occurred in the meeting we observed, and feelings and opinions were aired and dealt with during the meeting. Members were willing to be open with each other, and the resulting atmosphere encouraged clear and honest expression. The group listened to a number of alternatives and arrived at a final decision through consensus rather than by voting or imposition from above, partly because they took enough time to explore their own feelings, ideas, and opinions, listen to others, and modify their own positions when this seemed useful. There was no need for a scene II because the important action was played out in scene I. The members of the group didn't have gripes and complaints to air after the meeting, because the meeting itself was a place where opinions could be expressed. School Z's training in analyzing and practicing useful verbal behavior paid off in more productive staff meetings.

Improving Group Productivity

There is a wide variety of helpful behaviors one can utilize in group meetings, and many of these behaviors must be consciously learned. That is, many of us do not own these behaviors naturally—we must quite consciously acquire and practice them at first. As we "try on" new behaviors, and as we want to use them to improve our participation in groups and further the work of the groups in which we are involved, we will begin to adopt these new behaviors rather naturally. No matter how natural behavior may become, however, we will *always* need to be conscious of how we are participating in groups and of how others are behaving, if the groups in which we work are to be productive and satisfying.

In group meetings it is common for participants to share ideas or opinions and to ask others to further explain what they have introduced. Most people do not think of sharing feelings, however, or of summarizing what has happened or bringing in persons who have not participated or helping the group continue to explore alternatives rather than quickly latch on to the first workable solution offered. Many people actually interfere with the work of the group, without necessarily meaning to do so, by dominating the conversation and preventing others from participating or by attempting to smother controversy which needs to surface and be faced before any workable solutions can be achieved. The first activities presented in this chapter will help you take a look at some possible group behaviors and will offer opportunities to practice a variety of roles. The other exercises will help you practice listening skills; look at competition and collaboration; and plan for needed change in groups, organizations, or personal relations in which you are involved.

Group Membership Roles

The following list of group roles is presented in three parts. The first has to do with behaviors that further the work, or task, of the group, the second has to do with maintaining the group as a smoothly functioning unit; and the third defines some roles called personal, because they cater to self-oriented needs which interfere with the work of the group.[1]

---

[1] This material is based on the work of K. D. Benne and P. Sheats, "Functional Roles of Group Members," *Journal of Social Issues*, Vol. 4, No. 2,

Group Task Behavior:
Conduct That Furthers the Work of the Group

1. Initiating   Proposes aims, ideas, action, or procedures
2. Informing   Asks for or offers facts, ideas, feelings, or opinions
3. Clarifying   Illuminates or builds upon ideas or suggestions
4. Summarizing   Pulls data together, so group may consider where it is
5. Consensus Testing   Explores whether group may be nearing a decision; prevents premature decision-making

Group Maintenance Behavior:
Conduct That Helps the Group Function Productively

1. Harmonizing   Reconciles disagreements, relieves tension, helps people explore differences
2. Gate Keeping   Brings others in, suggests facilitating procedures, keeps communication channels open
3. Encouraging   Is warm and responsive; indicates with words or facial expression that the contributions of others are accepted
4. Compromising   Modifies position so group may move ahead; admits error
5. Giving Feedback   Tells others, in helpful ways, how their behavior is received

---

(Spring 1948), pp. 42–47. The listing of group task and group maintenance roles can be found, in somewhat different form from the way they are presented in this chapter, in the *Reading Book of the NTL Institute for Applied Behavioral Science,* 1201 Sixteenth Street, N.W., Washington, D.C., 1969, pp. 22–23.

Personal or Self-Oriented Behavior:
Conduct That Interferes with the Work of the Group

1. Aggressing   Attacks, deflates, uses sarcasm
2. Blocking   Resists beyond reason, uses hidden agenda items which prevent group movement
3. Dominating   Interrupts, asserts authority, overparticipates to point of interfering with others' participation
4. Avoiding   Prevents group from facing controversy; stays off subject to avoid commitment
5. Abandoning   Makes an obvious display of lack of involvement

Exercises in Observing, Analyzing, and Changing Group Behavior

POP: Process Observation Practice

Divide into separate groups of participants and observers. If your room is small, you may have to have just one group of about ten participants, with everyone else observing (taking turns, so that observers may also, at some time, become participants). If your room is large enough so that several different conversations can be easily heard, you can have a number of groups going at one time, with eight or ten participants, and a like number of observers. Observers may operate in one of several ways:

1. Each observer may select a certain participant to observe, and concentrate on him, noting into which category each of his statements fall.
2. All observers may note all behaviors of the entire group of participants.
3. One third of the observers may note all task behavior,

one third may tally maintenance behavior, and the other third will watch for self-oriented behavior in participants.

If the decision is to watch the behavior of several persons, it will be useful to put tally marks for each participant's statement using a sheet marked out as here, with the initials of the participants at the top and the behavior at the side.

	B.H.	L.C.	C.B.	D.R.	S.W.
Task Behavior 1. Initiating					
2. Informing					
3. Clarifying					
and so on . . .					

The participants will discuss a topic which calls for solutions or decisions and one which will provoke differing opinions. Any current local, national, or international problem may be used; and problems that are particularly relevant to the discussants are always appropriate; for example:

1. The assignments in this course should consist of
   _____.

2. The method of grading and evaluation in this course (my school, education in general) should be
   _____.

3. The education department (this college, our schools) would be vastly improved if _____.

Allow twenty to thirty minutes for this discussion.

Observers will give feedback to participants, using the data they have gathered based on group membership roles. More time will be required for total group feedback (all observers together giving feedback to all participants) than if one observer talks with one participant. You might allow ten to fifteen minutes for total group feedback or four to five minutes for individual feedback.

Participants will continue their group discussion for fifteen to twenty minutes more, this time trying for new behavior. For example, if a participant does not usually do any gate-keeping or encouraging, he might try these.

There will be a second feedback period. This time, even if observers are concentrating on individuals, allow some time for talking about the performance of the total group.

Switch, so that observers become participants, and vice versa. It is usual to continue the same topic of conversation, but this is not necessary.

Behavior by the Label

About ten participants will sit in a circle. There will be a sign in front of each, with one or two role behaviors written on both the front and back (so all can see). For example, one person's label may say "summarize" and "clarify"; another's may say "give feedback" and "encourage"; another, "dominate"; another, "abandon the group" (obviously engage in daydreaming, read a newspaper, back chair away from the group and look out the window, and so on). Those playing self-oriented roles should not overdo them to the point of parody but should make them realistic. Everyone else will observe.

Select a topic and discuss it for about ten minutes.

After the ten minutes is up, everybody will move one seat to the right and take on a new role according to the sign now in front of him. The discussion will continue for ten more minutes.

Everyone will switch one seat to the right once more and continue for ten more minutes.

Spend ten minutes or so discussing how the participants felt in the various roles.

Process Observation, On and On

Every time you have a class discussion of any length (or a faculty meeting, or, in fact, any meeting of an on-going group) ask one or two persons to serve as process observers and allow five to ten minutes at the end of the discussion for feedback on behavior. This is particularly worthwhile because you will receive feedback about your behavior in real situations.

Process Observation for the Private Eye

Whenever you are in a group of any kind, try to observe what is going on by noting the various roles that people play. You can observe process in any group: work groups, social groups, family groups, and so on.

For Children

The same categories for looking at group behavior can be used with children, though perhaps the terminology should be changed. For example:

Work Behavior

1. Has new ideas or suggestions
2. Asks for or gives information
3. Helps to explain better
4. Pulls ideas together
5. Finds out if the group is ready to decide what to do

Helping Behavior

1. Helps people get together
2. Brings other people in
3. Shows interest and kindness
4. Is willing to change own ideas to help group
5. Tells others in good ways how they are behaving

Troublesome Behavior

1. Attacks other people
2. Won't go along with other people's suggestions

3. Talks too much
4. Keeps people from discussing, because does not like arguments
5. Shows that he does not care about what is happening

(See Chapter 6 for an example of the use of this instrument with youngsters.)

A Listening Exercise

Divide into groups of from five to ten persons, depending upon how many groups can operate in your room and still be heard. The smaller the space, the smaller the groups have to be in order for conversation to be heard. This exercise may be carried out with the total group; however, the larger the group, the fewer opportunities there will be to participate.

Select any topic for discussion which is controversial and in which participants are interested. A current political or education issue or a class or college issue is suitable.

Anyone may begin the discussion and say whatever he wishes to say on the topic. The second person to speak must repeat the essence of what the first person has said—that is, he doesn't have to give a verbatim repetition, just the main idea or ideas. Then he must check out with the first speaker to be sure he has repeated correctly. A nod from the first speaker or an "okay" will be enough of a sign to indicate that the message has been correctly interpreted.

The second speaker may then go on and state his own point of view.

When the second speaker finishes, the third speaker must repeat what the second speaker has said and check out with him before he can go on to have his say. Each speaker repeats *only* the message of the person immediately preceding him, and anyone may speak—do *not* take set turns around the circle. If a person cannot repeat what was said before, he is not permitted to offer his own point of view.

Here is a sample of what might occur. The topic: *Women are the most oppressed human beings on earth.*

"Well, I don't believe that women are oppressed at all, so I think the topic is silly. Women have as much chance as anyone else; in fact, they have it better than men in many ways because they are more apt to have their own way, be supported by someone else, and, in general, be taken care of."

"You said that you don't think women are oppressed, and the topic is silly, and, in fact, women in many ways are better off than men, because they have their own way and so on. Okay? Well, I don't agree with you, I think that women are terribly oppressed, and to make things worse, most of them don't even know that they are oppressed. It's true that women aren't necessarily poor and they have as much in the way of food, shelter, and clothing as men, but they are definitely discriminated against in other ways. They are taught from birth that they are inferior to men—but they are also taught that this is a good thing!"

"You said that you think women are very much an oppressed group, and what makes their oppression even worse than it might be otherwise is that they are taught that it's good to be discriminated against in the ways that they are. Well, I agree, and I'll give you an example, which I heard just today. Some women were talking together before my last class, and one asked another what kind of list she had been making, saying that she appeared to be so well organized. The other said she was figuring out her checkbook, and the first said—*proudly,* mind you!—that her husband didn't allow her to fiddle with their checkbook! She was delighted to think that she was so feminine she didn't have a mind adequate to deal with figures!"

"Well, you said that you agree that women are oppressed, and you gave an example of a woman who was proud to say that her husband, in essence, told her she was too stupid to have access to their checkbook. I also think that women *are* really discriminated against, and I also believe that in most instances they are so brainwashed that they don't even know that their lives could be different. They think it's a mark of honor and success to be known as Mrs. John Smith rather than to have a name and identity of their own!"

"But that's ridiculous and anyway why shouldn't . . ."

"Wait a minute! you didn't repeat."

"Oh, yes. Well, you said that women are brainwashed and . . . well, I can't remember, so I guess I don't get a turn."

"Well, she said that women are so brainwashed that they don't realize that they are oppressed, and they don't realize that they don't even have the same degree of identity that men do. Well, I disagree, and I believe that women are not brainwashed, and what's more I believe that women dominate this country. Everybody knows that American women are very bossy and they run the men, not the other way around. Besides, how can they be the most oppressed group when there are people who are actually *starving* or who can't live in certain neighborhoods!"

"Boy! Where have you been lately! Women . . ."

"You didn't repeat what I said . . ."

For Children

This listening exercise may be used for short periods of time with even young children. (See Chapter 6 for examples of its use with fifth graders.)

The Game of Life[2]

This is a game to be played by six groups. A group may have as few as two members, but each group should have approximately the same number of players. The simplest way to make groups for this exercise is to have the total group count off by sixes, and then each person will join with all those holding the same number. That is, all the 1's will become a group, all the 2's, and so on. One person must remain out to act as the control person, to be the timekeeper, observer, and scorekeeper.

Object: Win as much as you can.

Procedure: This learning experience is like a game and has ten plays. On every play each group chooses either "Y" or "X" without necessarily knowing what the other groups have

---

[2] There are many variations of this game. This particular one was introduced to me by Dr. William Gellerman, an independent consultant in New York City.

chosen and writes its choice on a slip of paper. All slips are handed to the control person, who tallies them and announces the results. For example, if four groups have chosen "X" and two have chosen "Y," control will say, "X's win $4, Y's lose $8."

After plays four, six, and ten there will be a ten minute discussion and negotiation session at which one representative from each group will be present. The representatives discuss whatever they wish to. This representative may change from session to session or may be the same person each time. The sessions will be held out of the hearing of the groups, and the control person will serve as observer. *This game may seem complicated, but as you play you will see that it is easily understood.* Each group's payoff (winning or losing) depends on the combination of all six choices.

Payoff Possibilities:

choices	payoffs
All choose X	All lose $2
Five choose X One chooses Y	X's win $2 Y's lose $10
Four choose X Two choose Y	X's win $4 Y's lose $8
Three choose X Three choose Y	X's win $6 Y's lose $6
Two choose X Four choose Y	X's win $8 Y's lose $4
One chooses X Five choose Y	X wins $10 Y's lose $2
All choose Y	All win $2

Score Sheet

approximate time	play	check one		payoff	
		X	Y	won	lost
5 minutes	1				
3 minutes	2				
3 minutes	3				
3 minutes	4				
5 minutes*	5†				
3 minutes	6				
5 minutes*	7‡				
3 minutes	8				
3 minutes	9				
5 minutes*	10§				

	Total won	
	Total lost	
SCORE:	Won minus lost	

* These plays are preceded by a negotiation session.
† The payoff doubles on this play.
‡ The playoff triples.
§ The payoff is multiplied by ten.

When the Game Is Over

This game was described as a learning experience. Discuss as a total group what you have learned. Some things you might consider are:

1. What does "you" mean?
2. What were some of your feelings about winning and losing?
3. What were some of your feelings about competing and collaborating?
4. What analogies can you draw between this game and life in classrooms?
5. Compare what the winnings of the *total* group might have been with what they actually were.

For Children

This game can be played with children, but you will have to decide, as always, whether or not your particular class is old enough to benefit from the experience. You may want to simplify the rules by doing away with doubling and tripling winnings, and you might also want to have a negotiation session after *every* play, changing negotiators. This would help everyone to understand the implications of the playing of X's or Y's.

A Negotiation Exercise

This activity, like the previous one, will help you understand some of your feelings and behavior with respect to competition and collaboration.

Select one of the following topics for discussion:

1. The five most important topics that should be dealt with in school faculty meetings this year, in order of importance.
2. The eight most important qualities of a good teacher, ranked in order of importance.
3. The six topics this class should cover during the rest of the semester, in order of importance.

Decide quickly which topic to deal with. You may want to select a completely different topic, but it should be one that involves ranking. All of the groups must discuss the same topic.

Divide into groups of not less than six or seven numbers. Each group decides upon two of its members to be process observers. These two people will not participate in the discussion of the group, they will *observe* behavior. In addition to observing group maintenance, task, and personal behaviors, as explained in the first exercise in this chapter, the process observers will also note:

1. Who talks to whom
2. Who participates a lot, a little, not at all
3. How decisions are made

Discuss the chosen topic for twenty to thirty minutes and rank your choices as a group.

Receive feedback from your process observers for about ten to fifteen minutes. You may discuss their observations with them, but be sure to allow them enough time to tell you what they have observed.

Select one person from your discussion group to act as your representative in a negotiation session with representatives from each of the other groups. The negotiators will have from fifteen to twenty minutes to arrive at a final and joint ranking. In addition to a negotiator, select a floor manager—a person who will take messages between your negotiator and your group during the negotiation session. Only floor managers may speak to or exchange written messages with the negotiators.

Process observers should continue their observations—one from each group watching the negotiators and one concentrating on the behavior of his group.

The negotiators will meet in the center of the room, where everyone may observe their discussion, and within the time limit (fifteen or twenty minutes, approximately) they must arrive at a final listing and ranking.

At the conclusion of the negotiation session, the process observers will give feedback to the negotiators for about ten minutes.

The small groups will meet together once more to discuss their feelings about their commitment to their original list, the final results, their negotiator's role, and competition and collaboration. Take some time for a total group discussion of the activity.

For Children

This is a fine exercise for children, and some possible topics for them might be:

1. The four areas we would like to study this year, in order of importance.
2. The six most important characteristics of a friend, ranked in order of importance.
3. Eight things necessary in an ideal school, ranked in order of importance.

When discussing something that can actually be done, it is important for the results be carried through, as, for example, deciding areas for study.

Force-Field Analysis

This exercise is based upon the work of Kurt Lewin,[3] who theorized that every individual has a life space, or field; that each individual has certain goals which he seeks to achieve; and that there may be barriers to these goals which force a change in the field, in the goals, or in both. Change occurs when the driving forces, those that impel a person toward a certain goal, outweigh the effect of restraining forces, or those that prevent the achievement of the goal. Field theory, stated here in extremely simplified terms, can be applied to groups and organizations as well as to individuals.

[3] "Frontiers in Group Dynamics," *Human Relations,* Vol. 1 (1947), pp. 5–41.

To illustrate how this theory may be used in problem identification and solution, we will follow the work of a committee formed in a school that has severe problems with so-called disruptive children—youngsters who roam the classrooms and halls, destroy school property, pick on other children, both verbally and physically, and are often several years behind in most school subjects—children who are extremely difficult for teachers, administrators, and other pupils to work with. The committee's task is to figure out how to work more effectively with these children, and they decide to use a problem-identification technique, sometimes called a force-field analysis, to help them analyze the forces that are preventing them from operating more efficiently as a total school.

First, the committee tried to define the problem by stating as precisely as possible what their school situation was at the present time. They noted, for example, that many children weren't learning, that classes were often disrupted so severely that other youngsters were prevented from learning, that most teachers and administrators in the school could not handle the children, and that teachers were becoming more and more demoralized. Then they tried to describe their school as they would like it to be, stating that they would want all the youngsters in their school to attend regularly, to be interested in learning, to achieve at least the equivalent of national norms, to look forward to spending the day in school, and so on.

Their third step was to list all of the driving forces which might help them to achieve this ideal school—the existence of their committee; the fact that matters had attained such crisis proportions that something had to be done; that the methods now being used, like punishment, banishment, or simply ignoring the youngsters whenever this was possible, were failing completely; that the principal was very much in favor of change; that many members of the community were eager for change and would back them; that many of the teachers wanted to try new ways; and that there were some funds available for new materials and consultant help.

After they had listed all of the driving forces, their fourth step was to list all of the restraining forces they could think of—

such as the difficulty in keeping equipment from being stolen or destroyed; apathy on the part of some of the teachers and much of the community; the feelings of anger and distrust present in many of the children; the anger and hostility in many of the teachers; an old building that was particularly unattractive physically.

When they had listed all of the restraining and driving forces, the committee put asterisks next to those that were particularly critical, squares next to those that were most difficult to deal with, and triangles next to those that would most easily lend themselves to change.

The sixth step was to brainstorm possible solutions around each of the forces that were singled out in step five. That is, they suspended judgment and generated as many solutions as possible, however wild they might seem. No time was spent evaluating the effectiveness of the solutions—all ideas were acceptable. The solutions were aimed at reducing or eliminating restraining forces and expanding driving forces. Some of the ideas generated are given here: having kids make equipment, or shop themselves for the equipment; doing away with equipment; using the school only as a meeting place first thing in the morning and moving out into the city for the rest of the day; taking every class to the country for a week of fun and camping; paying kids to attend school and behave; transfering all teachers who didn't want to go along with the new plans; letting each class renovate their room in any way they wanted; paying teachers according to pupil attendance and making attendance optional.

The seventh and eighth steps were to decide upon which suggestions were to be worked on and to actually arrive at some plan of action. The committee decided exactly what actions they would recommend be taken to move from the situation they were in now to a situation that would be more like their ideal school. For example, they decided that there would be training sessions for teachers and administrators, with pupils included after the first few meetings, aimed at exploring and dealing with anger. They decided to have an interior decorating week, when plans would be made and carried out for painting and rearranging the school rooms and corridors and which would involve all pupils as well as all faculty. They decided to set up three rooms where disruptive children could be sent and where they would get plenty of attention from adults—and here they would use volunteers from the community and from the nearby college, as well as some professional teachers. The emphasis would be on learning, not punishment, and while pupils would be encouraged to return to their own classrooms when ready, they would not be punished for leaving or shamed for staying. Teachers would be encouraged to modify the usual curriculum in any way they felt would be helpful to their children, and youngsters would help plan curricula. There were other plans, but this is enough to give you an idea of how a force-field analysis can be used.

Using Force-Field Analysis To Identify and Solve Problems

The force-field analysis is a tool to help solve personal problems, group problems, or organizational problems and you should attempt to use it in all three contexts. For example, you might go through the steps to work on a problem you are having and compare notes in pairs or trios afterwards. You might get together with several persons and work on a group problem—preferably a real one. It may be that you will want to use this problem-solving exercise with some outside group of which you are a member and then report on the results of your efforts to others in your class. You might work in several small groups on a common class or school problem. But try to use this technique to solve a personal, a group, *and* an organizational problem. Here are the steps to follow:

1. Define your problem as precisely as possible. Spend enough time so that you really determine what your problem is. Sometimes the problem you think exists is not the true problem, and you may discover this as you attempt to state your problem definitively.

2. Try to describe what things would look like if your problem were solved. What would your life (or your organization) be like?

3. Share your results so far with another individual or another small group, helping each other where possible.

4. List all of the forces that are driving you toward the solution of your problem—all the helpful forces in your field, or life space.

5. List all of the forces that are restraining you from solving your problem—from arriving at the place where you want to be.

6. Share your results again.

7. Take your driving forces and star those that are particularly critical and add triangles next to those you think you can capitalize upon.

8. Take your list of restraining forces and star those that seem especially important; add triangles next to those you think you can change most readily; and put squares next to those you think you would have the most difficulty changing.

9. Select the driving forces that seem most capable of being capitalized upon and brainstorm as many solutions as you can for each one, without regard to feasibility. If working in a group, build on each other's wild ideas; the more ideas you generate here, the better. Quantity rather than quality is sought at this time.

10. Select the restraining forces you believe can be changed or eliminated and brainstorm possible actions for each of these.

11. Decide which actions and solutions from your brainstorming list are worthwhile. Look for what may be sound in even the wildest of schemes.

12. Draw up a plan of action that will take you from where you are now to where you want to be.
13. Share with another group.
14. Set a specific time for evaluating the progress you are making, or have made—for example, two weeks from today, six months from today.

For Children

This activity can certainly be used with children, but once again you will want to change some of the terminology or shorten the exercise, depending upon your particular class.

This entire book is based upon the premise that you *can* change your behavior, but remember *you* are the only person who can make changes in yourself. Others can tell you what you're like and how you make them feel, but the decisions about whether or not you want to change are up to you. Putting the decisions into action are also up to you. The next chapter will deal with classroom talk and you will face some decisions about your own verbal behavior, its effect on others in the classroom, and changes you might want to make.

Selected References

The Journal of Applied Behavioral Science, NTL Institute for Applied Behavioral Science, 1201 Sixteenth Street, N.W., Washington, D.C. 20036.

Donald Nylen, J. Robert Mitchell, and Anthony Stout. *Handbook of Staff Development and Human Relations Training: Material Developed for Use in Africa,* NTL Institute for Applied Behavioral Science, 1201 Sixteenth Street, N.W., Washington, D.C. 20036.

J. William Pfeiffer and John E. Jones. *A Handbook of Structured Experiences for Human Relations Training,* Vol. I,

II and III, University Associates Press, P.O. Box 615, Iowa City, Iowa 52240, 1969, 1970, 1971.

10 Interaction Exercises for the Classroom, NTL Institute for Applied Behavioral Science, 1201 Sixteenth Street, N.W., Washington, D.C. 20036.

4 talk, talk, talk

Since this is a book about the ways in which people behave with one another in schools, and since a great deal of teaching-learning behavior consists of talk, this chapter and the next focus on verbal interaction. The material to be presented is designed to help you notice how teachers and pupils talk to each other, provide you with opportunities to practice new ways of speaking, and help you select and internalize that verbal behavior which you would like to have as your own. You found with the various group roles presented in Chapter 3 that there are certain behaviors you do not "own" but would like to acquire, and, you also discovered that you need consciously to practice over and over again the behaviors that you want to own, if you are ever to use them easily at appropriate times. The new behaviors may feel uncomfortable at first, but if you believe that certain kinds of talk are useful to have in your repertory, and you continue to try them, you will begin to own them naturally and easily. It is important to remember, however, that in order to select appropriate verbal behavior for each situation and each child, you will *always* need to be acutely conscious of your own talk and that of your pupils. In other words, in order to teach as effectively as possible you will always need to act on the basis of intelligent choice rather than in haphazard or routine ways.

While we will be concentrating our energies in this chapter and the next on talk, nonverbal behavior is also important. Frowns, smiles, body stances which slump with discouragement or say, it's nice to be alive, a friendly arm placed about the shoulder of another or an angry hand grasping another's arm— all of these enhance or impede human communication. Galloway[1] has developed a system for observing teacher nonverbal behavior which includes categories for actions and facial expressions covering a range of feelings from enthusiastic support through inattention to outright disapproval. In this book we are focusing on verbal behavior, however, because talk and tone of voice are usually consistent with nonverbal behavior, and because talk, in addition to making up such a large portion of teaching and learning behavior, is more amenable to observation and practice than are gestures and facial expressions.

There is a great deal of current research which analyzes the verbal behavior of teachers and pupils, and there are many interesting and helpful systems for studying classroom talk.[2] One

[1] Charles H. Galloway, "Categories for Observing Teacher Nonverbal Communication," in Ronald T. Hyman (ed.), *Teaching: Vantage Points for Study* (Philadelphia: J. B. Lippincott Company, 1968), pp. 74–77.
[2] Anita Simon and E. Gil Boyer (eds.), *Mirrors for Behavior: An Anthology of Classroom Observation Instruments* (Philadelphia: Research for Better Schools, 1700 Market Street, January 1968 and Spring 1970).

of the best known and most widely used of these systems was developed by Flanders,[3] who divides classroom talk into ten categories. Flanders' first seven categories are for teacher talk and consist of acceptance of feeling, praise, acceptance of ideas, questions, lecture, giving directions, and criticism. His eighth and ninth categories are for pupils and are labeled pupil response and pupil initiation; and there is a tenth category which is for silence or confusion. The categories are numbered so that an observer may listen to classroom talk and tally a number every three seconds according to which category is occurring. These numbers are then entered on a matrix, which provides an objective picture of what occurred in the classroom during a certain lesson, according to the Flanders categories. The teacher who has been observed (and teachers can evaluate themselves by using audio or video tapes of their own teaching) can then use the matrix to learn, for example, what percentage of the time he talked compared with his pupils; whether he followed pupil contributions with praise, with acceptance, or with criticism; whether the questions he asked were broad enough to be followed by extended pupil response or were of the narrow sort which can be answered in a few words.

In an earlier book,[4] my co-author and I developed the Verbal Interaction Category System, or VICS, which was based upon the Flanders system but contained additional categories. I have further revised this system and named it the FLICS; it is used in this chapter and the next in order to help you become conscious of classroom talk and to help you practice and modify your own talk and that of your pupils. The FLICS is outlined in Table 1.

[3] Ned A. Flanders, *Analyzing Teaching Behavior* (Reading, Mass.: Addison-Wesley Publishing Company, Inc., 1970).
[4] Edmund Amidon and Elizabeth Hunter, *Improving Teaching: The Analysis of Classroom Verbal Interaction* (New York: Holt, Rinehart and Winston, Inc., 1966).

TABLE 1

The FLICS

Hunter Revision of Flanders Interaction Analysis Categories

teacher talk

1. ACCEPTS FEELING: acknowledges the existence of feelings by reflecting, clarifying, or identifying. "You feel upset." "You feel angry because you believe you were unfairly treated." "I understand how you feel," or "People often cry when they're hurt."
2. PRAISES:
   (a) using no reason or personal approval without further reason. "Good." "I like that."
   (b) using rational reason. "This quiet atmosphere helps those of us working in small groups." "You figured out a good way of fitting another character in, so now everyone can have a part."
3. ACCEPTS IDEAS: by repeating, acknowledging, summarizing, clarifying, or developing.
4. ASKS QUESTIONS, which involve: (categories are taken from the work of Gallagher and Aschner)
   (a) recall: involves facts and rote memory; is narrow. "What is the name of the game we played yesterday?"
   (b) comprehension: calls for the processing of given or remembered data through analysis or integration. Answers can be right or wrong. "What are some differences between that game and dodge ball?"
   (c) invention: calls for answers that are creative and imaginative, that move in new directions. "What are some ways you could change this game so it would be more fun?" No one right answer.
   (d) evaluation: calls for judgment and choice. May be broad or narrow. "Do you like this game?" "What are

some reasons why this might or might not be a good game for adults and children to play together?" "Do you think games are as important as reading, and if so, why?"

(e) routine: concerned with management. "Are we ready?" "Any questions?"

5. GIVES INFORMATION OR OPINION: presents content or own ideas, explains, asks rhetorical questions. Can be short statements or extended lecture.

6. GIVES DIRECTION: tells pupils to take specific actions, gives orders. (h) harshly

7. CRITICIZES OR REJECTS IDEAS, FEELINGS, BEHAVIOR:
   (a) using no reason or personal disapproval without further reasons. "Wrong." "I don't want you to do that."
   (b) using rational reasons: "Your answer is wrong because you forgot to add in the last three numbers." "You shouldn't be talking—we can't hear each other." (h) harshly

pupil talk

8. RESPONDS TO TEACHER: pupil talk in direct response to any teacher solicitation. Responses may be incorrect.

9. INITIATES TALK TO TEACHER: speaks to teacher on own initiative.

10. TALKS TO TOTAL CLASS OR INDIVIDUAL PUPILS: *true* group discussion (which can include teacher) or interaction betweeen one or more pupils.

other

11. SILENCE—during periods of discussion. Not tallied during seat work time, for example.

Z. CONFUSION: noise which interferes with class work. If regular discussion can still be followed, tally Z's alongside other categories.

Developed by Elizabeth Hunter.

Before we examine the FLICS in more detail, let's listen to two discussions in two different undergraduate teacher education classrooms.

Talk in Classrooms

Classroom I

"The chapter we read for today, class, says, in essence, that teachers need not be terribly concerned with the social or emotional aspects of education—that schools are places where cognitive learning is meant to occur, and that teachers are not and should not act as psychologists. What do you think about that?" asked Mr. Connally, the class instructor.

There was a pause of ten or fifteen seconds. Mr. Connally did not restate the question; he looked pleasantly around at the class.

"Well," Joe Pennell spoke up, "I think the author is right. The schools *are* the institutions where kids come to learn to read and to learn history and literature, and there really isn't any other place for them to go for this kind of learning. For social learnings they can join the Scouts or a hundred and one other organizations."

"In the neighborhood where I'm student teaching there aren't a hundred and one other places to go," said Walt Schultz. "There's school, home, and the streets, and that's it. However, I agree with you that teachers should concentrate on the cognitive aspects of schooling. Not that we shouldn't be aware of feelings and things like that, but they're secondary."

"So you're both saying that you agree with the point of view of the author—that the main business of the schools, and therefore of teachers, is to transmit cognitive learning, and that this is particularly important since society provides no other place for youngsters to learn much of what is incorporated in the school curriculum," summarized the instructor.

"Well, I don't deny that schools ought to be concerned with things like reading and history and literature, but I certainly can't agree that the social and emotional aspects of schooling are *less* important. I'm not saying they're more important than the cognitive, but I would definitely rate them as equally important. Certainly there's a lot of evidence that pupils learn more in classrooms where the emotional climate is supportive and where teachers care about kids," declared Lucy Rodriquez.

"I disagree with the author completely," said Betty Brown. "Teachers need to be more concerned with the social and emotional aspects of learning than with the cognitive precisely because it's so obvious that most school time is spent learning subjects like reading and spelling and math. There's no getting away from that, and no thought, really of getting away from that—it's just built-in. So teachers automatically *have* to be concerned with that. Which says to me that teachers *need* to be more aware of the social and emotional aspects of schooling, because they're of such tremendous importance in learning, and because they are not obviously included—to be 'covered' like the usual subjects."

"We've heard some views now which differ from those of the first two speakers," said Mr. Connally. "Lucy and Betty feel that teachers do need to concern themselves with the affective aspects of education, and Betty feels that affect may be especially important for teachers to be concerned with because it's not automatically built into the school curriculum, yet is so inextricably tied up with cognitive learning."

"I feel as Betty does," Charles Linton joined in. "The more I go around and observe in schools, the more I think it would be better for schools to be places where kids *want* to be rather than places where they learn a lot of facts, most of which they promptly forget."

"Wait a minute! Who's talking about learning facts?" asked Jay Lerner. "You make it sound as though learning academic subjects is automatically uninvolving and boring, and I certainly don't go along with that. No subject ought to be concerned only with presenting facts, and every subject can be interesting if presented well and boring if presented poorly. All we have to do is look at our own college courses to know that. So if the cognitive stuff is presented well, you'll feel good about the subject and about school and you'll learn, and if it's presented in a boring way, you won't."

"Right," Angie James chimed in. "Remember when we had that discussion about raising kids' levels of self-esteem and some people said they would accomplish this by letting kids go on errands, wash the boards, empty the wastebaskets, and things like that? Well, when you spend the day learning that you're a terrible reader and that you can't spell or do math, it won't do very much good to go on a few errands for the teacher so you can feel good about yourself! School is about learning certain subjects, and that's what teachers have to be concerned about— teaching those subjects well so that kids learn."

"You know, it annoys me to hear people say that it's more important to deal with feelings in school than with cognition, or vice versa," said Ed Thomas rather vehemently. "How can you separate the two? Everybody knows that feelings are bound up with everything we do and that knowledge isn't transmitted in some sort of sterile place uncontaminated by feelings."

"Well, *I* certainly didn't say that feelings are more important or less important than knowledge," Betty Brown responded. "If you bothered to listen to me you would have heard me say that all of us will *have* to deal with cognition, but we'll need to make a special effort to remember to be concerned with affect."

"You both seem to have strong feelings about this issue," said Mr. Connally.

"Yes, I *do* feel strongly about this," replied Betty. "And I'd like to say again that I in no way deny the importance of academic subjects. I agree that if they aren't presented well, then forget it! However, there are lots of things that go on in schools that don't have anything to do with the actual teaching of academic subjects, like how Susie and Jane get along and the fact that Jimmy is exhausted because he never gets enough sleep and that Bob can't pay attention no matter how fascinating things are because his parents are splitting up! And that stuff isn't in the curriculum guide."

"Okay, okay," said Ed Thomas. "I don't disagree with you. When I say that cognition and affect are bound together,

I know that affect isn't in the curriculum guide. But I look upon the kinds of problems you just brought up as legitimate areas for cognitive learning—just like reading or math."

"Mr. Connally, you've put a lot of emphasis on affect in this course," said Shirley Willette, "but so far today you haven't said anything about where you stand on this issue."

"Well, I guess I agree with a good deal of what's been said, even though some of the discussion seems to represent opposing points of view," answered Mr. Connally. "I believe that the main business of the school is to teach youngsters how to read and do math and think coherently, and in general to teach kids that learning can be exciting. I believe that children come to school thinking that learning is exciting and that if they stop feeling that way it's the school's fault. I also believe that the way in which subjects are taught, that is, the way teaching is, will have an overpowering effect on how these subjects are learned. And I believe that the learning of academic subjects is completely bound up with affect. I may be teaching math, but the manner I have as I teach is of tremendous importance in the learning; or I may be teaching human relations, which then becomes the cognitive subject matter, and my manner, or affect, is still of tremendous importance in what is learned."

"Well, it seems to me that if you know your subject, whether it's math or human relations, and if you're enthusiastic about it, then kids will be interested too, and will learn," said Hilda Marvel.

"I don't agree with that at all," said Charles Linton. "Someone said before that all we have to do is look at the courses we take in college to know that if stuff is presented well it will be interesting and if it isn't, it will be boring. Well we can look around at our courses here, Hilda, and see that there are lots of professors who are enthusiastic about their subjects and know a tremendous amount in their fields but who don't know anything about teaching and are very boring. Their students may cover the material for the exam, but that's not learning as far as I'm concerned."

"Jay, you said that stuff about courses which are presented in an interesting manner being interesting, and I'm not sure I even agree with that, if you're talking about lectures," said Gloria Jensen. "I've discovered that even when I think lectures are interesting at the time, I usually don't learn very much from them—when I think back about the content later. I do okay on the tests, perhaps, and I may look forward to going to the class more than I do to a dull lecture class, but I don't think that's good teaching. The professor could hand out the lecture on a mimeographed sheet and we could read it in one third the time."

"Well, I didn't mean just lecturing when I talked about getting kids excited about learning," responded Jay, "but I certainly think that as the person with the expertise, the teacher will have to do *some* lecturing."

"We all seem to agree that in order for kids to be interested in learning, teachers must present subject matter in stimulating ways," said Mr. Connally. "I'm going to suggest an exercise now in which we'll divide up into groups of four and pick some simple concept to teach—anything at all from any subject you're studying at this time. Then, take about fifteen minutes to plan a three to five minute presentation which will be interesting and involving and another presentation of the same length which will be dull. We need an equal number of groups, because when we're ready, each group will teach another group; first in the boring way and then in the interesting way. Any questions about what we're going to do? Okay, then, let's go."

Classroom II

"The chapter we read for today, class, says, in essence, that teachers must be concerned with the affective aspects of education as much as with the cognitive; that teachers, in other words, must be vitally concerned with the social and emotional aspects of learning. What do you think about that?" asked Mr. Harmon, the instructor.

When no one answered immediately, Mr. Harmon said, with evident sarcasm, "Come on, now, there must be several of the old faithfuls who have read the chapter. Should teachers be concerned with affect or not?"

"Well, yes and no," said Ellen Brody. "I . . . ."

"That's a pretty safe position!" said Mr. Harmon, and several class members tittered appreciatively.

"Well, that is, I mean, I do have a position," Ellen continued. "It seems to me that teachers need to be concerned with the social and emotional aspects of education and with the cognitive aspects as well."

"You're still pretty safe, and you haven't really said very much, I'm afraid," commented Mr. Harmon.

"I think teachers need to be concerned with affect, Mr. Harmon, but certainly not as much as with cognition. After all, that's what schools are all about," said Lonnie Voight.

"Now that's typical of the way people express ideas and opinions in this class—'that's what schools are all about'! Remember, please, that you're in a college classroom and you should be able to carry on adult discussions using adult language. I permit time for the exchange of ideas and I expect the time to be well used," scolded Mr. Harmon.

"Well, I mean," responded Lonnie, "that schools are supposed to be primarily concerned with teaching academic subjects, and so it's just common sense that teachers should be more concerned with the cognitive aspects of teaching."

"That's better. However, I can't say that I agree with your statement that because schools are mainly concerned with academic matters, teachers should logically be more concerned with cognition. Just because there is historically more stress in schools on academic subjects than on affect doesn't mean that social and emotional learnings are less important than cognitive learnings. Maybe teachers should start being leaders rather than followers and start concerning themselves with what they think is important, regardless of what present curricula say should be stressed."

There was another pause and Mr. Harmon said, "I'm beginning to wonder why I schedule these discussion times at all. Most of you don't seem to appreciate them. Mr. Thompson, what do you think?"

"Well, it seems to me that teachers need to be very much concerned with affect. It isn't enough to just lecture at the kids or have them read from their books and do workbook kinds of things. We must know what our pupils are like, what their interests are, what their problems are, and so on, so we can present subject matter in a variety of ways—so children will learn."

"Good! I'm glad to see that somebody is thinking! Anyone else?"

Again there was a period of silence and Mr. Harmon said, "I don't know what's wrong with this class! I don't believe most of you even bother to do the reading. Now before our next class session I expect every one of you to either reread the chapter or, more likely, read it for the first time, and I want a four-page paper from each of you on whether you think teachers should be more concerned with affect or with cognition. And you are to come to class prepared to engage in a *decent* discussion. After all, you aren't in high school anymore. Frankly, I don't know how you people expect to become teachers!"

An Analysis of the Talk in Classrooms I and II

The two classroom situations we have just read will be presented again, and this time each statement will be followed by a FLICS number and some discussion. Take a few minutes now to study the FLICS categories presented in Table 1; read them over carefully and become familiar with them. Then reread the situations as they are presented here.

Classroom I

"The chapter we read for today, class, says, in essence, that teachers need not be terribly concerned with the social or emotional aspects of education—that schools are places where cognitive learning is meant to occur and that teachers are not and should not act as psychologists. (5) *In this sentence the instructor briefly gives the class some information about the assigned chapter.* "What do you think about that?" (4b) asked Mr. Connally, the class instructor. *An evaluative question, one that solicits students' opinions, is asked.*

There was a pause (11) of ten or fifteen seconds. Mr. Connally did not restate the question; he looked pleasantly around at the class. *Since Mr. Connally has asked a question which requires thought, he permits time for this thought. Very often, teachers are uncomfortable with silence, and rather than wait it out will rephrase the question, often making it narrower ("Should schools spend more time on teaching reading or on teaching socialization?"), or they ask a different question, also often narrower ("What is the difference between social or emotional learning and cognitive learning?"), or they may answer the question themselves, or they may criticize the class for not answering immediately ("We've been over this before in other contexts, but you still don't seem able to deal with it!"). Thought-provoking questions require thinking time, and it's worth waiting through the silence, even though you may begin to feel anxious. After all, what is the worst thing that can happen? Silence and perhaps some embarrassment are not a very high price to pay, really, for giving time for thought. Naturally, if the silence extends for an unreasonable period you still have other behaviors available to you; but train yourself to wait through at least some period of silence after you ask provocative questions.*

"Well," Joe Pennell spoke up, "I think the author is right. The schools *are* the institutions where kids come to learn to read and to learn history and literature, and there really isn't any other place for them to go for this kind of learning. For social learnings they can join the Scouts or a hundred and one other organizations." (8) *This response to the question is rated as (8) rather than a (10) because we will assume the speaker is looking directly at the teacher and speaking primarily to him.*

"In the neighborhood where I'm student teaching there aren't a hundred and one other places to go," said Walt Schultz. "There's school, home, and the streets, and that's it. However, I agree with you that teachers should concentrate on the cognitive aspects of schooling. Not that we shouldn't be aware of feelings and things like that, but they're secondary." (10) *This pupil statement and all others in the discussion which are followed by 10's are tallied that way because the pupil is talking to the total class, including the teacher, or to one of more indi-*

vidual students—rather than only to the teacher. 10's are used for group discussions in which the participants are really talking to each other, a quite different arrangement from the more usual classroom situation in which all pupil talk is directed to the teacher and not to the group as a whole or to individual classmates.

"So you're both saying that you agree with the point of view of the author—that the main business of the schools, and therefore of teachers, is to transmit cognitive learnings and that this is particularly important since society provides no other place for youngsters to learn much of what is incorporated in the school curriculum" (3), summarized the instructor. *In this statement the instructor accepts the ideas of the two previous speakers by briefly summarizing what they have said.*

"Well, I don't deny that schools ought to be concerned with things like reading and history and literature, but I certainly can't agree that the social and emotional aspects of schooling are *less* important. I'm not saying they're more important than the cognitive, but I would definitely rate them as equally important. Certainly there's a lot of evidence that pupils learn more in classrooms where the emotional climate is supportive and where teachers care about kids" (10), declared Lucy Rodriquez.

"I disagree with the author completely," said Betty Brown. "Teachers need to be more concerned with the social and emotional aspects of learning than with the cognitive precisely because it's so obvious that most school time is spent learning subjects like reading and spelling and math. There's no getting away from that, and no thought, really, of getting away from that—it's just built-in. So teachers automatically *have* to be concerned with that. Which says to me that teachers *need* to be aware of the social and emotional aspects of schooling, because they're of such tremendous importance in learning and because they are not obviously included—to be 'covered' like the usual subjects." (10)

"We've heard some views now which differ from those of the first two speakers," said Mr. Connally. "Lucy and Betty feel that teachers do need to concern themselves with the affective aspects of education, and Betty feels that affect may be especially important for teachers to be concerned with because it's not automatically built into the school curriculum, yet is so inextricably tied up with cognitive learning." (3) *Once again the instructor accepts the ideas of the two previous speakers by briefly summarizing what they have said.*

"I feel as Betty does," Charles Linton joined in. "The more I go around and observe in schools, the more I think it would be better for schools to be places where kids *want* to be rather than places where they learn a lot of facts, most of which they promptly forget." (10)

"Wait a minute! Who's talking about learning facts?" asked Jay Lerner. "You make it sound as though learning academic subjects is automatically uninvolving and boring, and I certainly don't go along with that. No subject ought to be concerned only with presenting facts, and every subject can be interesting if presented well and boring if presented poorly. All we have to do is look at our own college courses to know that. So if the cognitive stuff is presented well, you'll feel good about the subject and about school and you'll learn, and if it's presented in a boring way, you won't." (10)

"Right," Angie James chimed in. "Remember when we had that discussion about raising kids' levels of self-esteem and some people said they would accomplish this by letting kids go on errands, wash the boards, empty the wastebaskets, and things like that? Well, when you spend the day learning that you're a terrible reader and that you can't spell or do math, it won't do very much good to go on a few errands for the teacher so you can feel good about yourself! School is about learning certain subjects, and that's what teachers have to be concerned about—teaching those subjects well so that kids learn." (10)

"You know, it annoys me to hear people say that it's more important to deal with feelings in school than with cognition, or vice versa," said Ed Thomas rather vehemently. "How can you separate the two? Everybody knows that feelings are bound up with everything that we do and that knowledge isn't transmitted in some sort of sterile place uncontaminated by feelings." (10)

Well, *I* certainly didn't say that feelings are more important or less important than knowledge," Betty Brown responded. "If you bothered to listen to me you would have heard me say that all of us will have to deal with cognition, but we'll need to make a special effort to remember to be concerned with affect." (10)

"You both seem to have strong feelings about this issue," (1) said Mr. Connally. *The instructor accepts or acknowledges the feelings expressed by reflecting what he hears as the pupils' strong feelings.*

"Yes, I do feel strongly about this," replied Betty. "And I'd like to say again that I in no way deny the importance of academic subjects. I agree that if they aren't presented well, then forget it! However, there are lots of things that go on in schools that don't have anything to do with the actual teaching of academic subjects, like how Susie and Jane get along and the fact that Jimmy is exhausted because he never gets enough sleep and that Bob can't pay attention no matter how fascinating things are because his parents are splitting up! And that stuff isn't in the curriculum guide. (10)

"Okay, okay," said Ed Thomas. "I don't disagree with you. When I say that cognition and affect are bound together, I know that affect isn't in the curriculum guide. But I look upon the kinds of problems you just brought up as legitimate areas for cognitive learning—just like reading or math." (10)

"Mr. Connally, you've put a lot of emphasis on affect in this course," said Shirley Willette, "but so far today you haven't said anything about where you stand on this issue." (9) *Here a student initiates talk to the instructor, asking him a question.*

"Well, I guess I agree with a good deal of what's been said, even though some of the discussion seems to represent opposing points of view," answered Mr. Connally. "I believe that the main business of the school is to teach youngsters how to read and do math and think coherently, and in general to teach kids that learning can be exciting. I believe that children come to school thinking that learning is exciting and that if they stop feeling that way it's the school's fault. I also believe that the way in which subjects are taught, that is, the way teaching is, will have an overpowering effect on how these subjects are learned. And I believe that the learning of academic subjects is completely bound up with affect. I may be teaching math, but the manner I have as I teach is of tremendous importance in the learning; or I may be teaching human relations, which then becomes the cognitive subject matter, and my manner, or affect, is still of tremendous importance in what is learned." (5) *The instructor responds to the pupil question by giving his opinions on the subject under discussion.*

"Well, it seems to me that if you know your subject, whether it's math or human relations, and if you're enthusiastic about it, then kids will be interested too, and will learn," said Hilda Marvel. (10)

"I don't agree with that at all," said Charles Linton. "Someone said before that all we have to do is look at the courses we take in college to know that if stuff is presented well it will be interesting and if it isn't, it will be boring. Well we can look around at our courses here, Hilda, and see that there are lots of professors who are enthusiastic about their subjects and know a tremendous amount in their fields but who don't know anything about teaching and are very boring. Their students may cover the material for the exam, but that's not learning as far as I'm concerned." (10)

"Jay, you said that stuff about courses which are presented in an interesting manner being interesting, and I'm not sure I even agree with that, if you're talking about lectures," said Gloria Jensen. "I've discovered that even when I think lectures are interesting at the time, I usually don't learn very much from them—when I think back about the content later. I do okay on the tests, perhaps, and I may look forward to going to the class more than I do to a dull lecture class, but I don't think that's good teaching. The professor could hand out the lecture on a mimeographed sheet and we could read it in one third the time." (10)

"Well, I didn't mean just lecturing when I talked about getting kids excited about learning," responded Jay, "but I certainly think that as the person with the expertise, the teacher will have to do *some* lecturing." (10)

"We all seem to agree that in order for kids to be interested in learning, teachers must present subject matter in stimulating ways," said Mr. Connally. (3) *In this sentence the instructor accepts the variously expressed opinions that teachers must present content in interesting ways.* "I'm going to suggest an exercise now in which we'll divide up into groups of four and pick some simple concept to teach—anything at all from any subject you're studying at this time. Then, take about fifteen minutes to plan a three to five minute presentation which will be interesting and involving and another presentation of the same length which will be dull. We need an equal number of groups, because when we're ready, each group will teach another group, first in the boring way and then in the interesting way. (6) *Mr. Connally gives the class directions about what they will be doing next.* Any questions about what we're going to do? (4e) *This is a routine question asked to check out class understanding of the activity.* Okay, then, let's go." (6) *The episode ends with the teacher giving a direction about the next activity.*

Classroom II

"The chapter we read for today, class, says, in essence, that teachers must be concerned with the affective aspects of education as much as with the cognitive; that teachers, in other words, must be vitally concerned with the social and emotional aspects of learning. (5) *The instructor gives information to the class.* What do you think about that?" (4d) asked Mr. Harmon, the instructor. *He follows this initial information-giving sentence with an evaluative question.*

When no one answered immediately, Mr. Harmon said, with evident sarcasm, "Come on, now, there must be several of the old faithfuls who have read the chapter. (7a) *Mr. Harmon does not wait for even three seconds to elapse after his question before criticizing the class by suggesting that many or most of them probably have not read the chapter.* "Should teachers be concerned with affect or not?" (4d) *The instructor rephrases the question, making it somewhat narrower, but still evaluative.*

"Well, yes and no," said Ellen Brody. "I . . ." (8)

"That's a pretty safe position!" (7a) said Mr. Harmon, and several class members tittered appreciatively. *The teacher criticizes the response, saying it's safe—which doesn't provide enough feedback about what's wrong with the answer to count as a rational reason for the criticism.*

"Well, that is, I mean, I do have a position," Ellen continued. "It seems to me that teachers need to be concerned with the social and emotional aspects of education and with the cognitive aspects as well." (8)

"You're still pretty safe, and you haven't really said very much, I'm afraid." (7a) commented Mr. Harmon. *Another criticism of the student response, still giving no reasons that would help the student understand how to improve.*

"I think teachers need to be concerned with affect, Mr. Harmon, but certainly not as much as with cognition. After all, that's what schools are all about." (8) said Lonnie Voight. *This student's talk and the others which follow are tallied as 8's rather than 10's because each student speaks directly to Mr. Harmon, and his talk encourages them to speak directly to him rather than engage in true group discussion.*

"Now that's typical of the way people express ideas and opinions in this class—'that's what schools are all about'! Remember, please, that you're in a college classroom and you should be able to carry on adult discussions using adult language. I permit time for the exchange of ideas, and I expect the time to be well used" (7ah), scolded Mr. Harmon. *Again Mr. Harmon criticizes without giving reasons as to why the contributions are unacceptable, beyond saying to "speak like adults," whatever that may mean. If he had said, "Your answer would be improved if you would tell us more exactly what you believe the job of the schools to be," that would be (7b). The tone of voice of the speaker is an indication of whether or not we would add an "h" for "harshly," and Mr. Harmon is not merely saying the response is wrong, he is castigating the speaker and the class—as well as indicating they do not appreciate what he is doing for them.*

"Well, I mean," responded Lonnie, "that schools are supposed to be primarily concerned with teaching academic subjects, and so it's just common sense that teachers should be more concerned with cognitive aspects of teaching." (8)

"That's better." (2a) *This time Mr. Harmon uses praise without reasons.* However, I can't say that I agree with your statement that because schools are mainly concerned with academic matters, teachers should logically be more concerned with cognition. Just because there is historically more stress in schools on academic subjects than on affect doesn't mean that social and emotional learnings are less important than cognitive learnings. (7b) *The teacher criticizes the response, saying why he doesn't think the response is as logical as it could be.* Maybe teachers should start being leaders rather than followers and start concerning themselves with what they think is important, regardless of what present curricula say should be stressed. (5) *Mr. Harmon states an idea of his own.*

There was another pause (11) *This is not a pause directly following a question, but probably results from the instructor's critical comments after almost every contribution—which would tend to make class members hesitate to speak.* and Mr. Harmon said, "I'm beginning to wonder why I schedule these discussion times at all. Most of you don't seem to appreciate them. (7a) *Mr. Harmon makes another criticizing comment without giving rational reasons.* Mr. Thompson, what do you think?" (4d) *The instructor asks the evaluative question again, this time calling on someone by name since no one volunteers.*

"Well, it seems to me that teachers need to be very much concerned with affect. It isn't enough to just lecture at the kids or have them read from their books and do workbook kinds of things. We must know what our pupils are like, what their interests are, what their problems are, and so on, so we can present subject matter in a variety of ways—so children will learn." (8)

"Good! I'm glad to see that somebody is thinking!" (2a) *Praise from Mr. Harmon, without any reasons as to why the comment is worthy of praise.* Anyone else?" (4d) *The instructor repeats the question again. The class is evidently still reluctant to talk. One person has received praise—but the teacher is so judgmental that members may not feel like taking risks.*

Again there was a period of silence (11) and Mr. Harmon said, "I don't know what's wrong with this class! I don't believe most of you even bother to do the reading. (7ah) *More criticism from the teacher.* Now before our next class session I expect every one of you to either reread the chapter or, more likely, read it for the first time, and I want a four-page paper from each of you on whether you think teachers should be more concerned with affect or with cognition. And you are to come to class prepared to engage in a decent discussion. (6ah) *Directions given harshly in a castigating manner.* After all, you aren't in high school anymore. Frankly, I don't know how you people expect to become teachers! (7ah) *Mr. Harmon concludes with criticism given without reason—just a generalized "you're not much good" sort of comment.*

It is clear that the behavior in these two classrooms was quite different. In the first classroom, the instructor encouraged pupils to speak and share their ideas by accepting their contributions. In the second classroom, the pupils were discouraged from participating by an instructor who criticized them, much of the time in a harsh manner, and who did not usually give any corrective information which would help them improve their contributions.

The FLICS Categories: Explanations and Skill Sessions

In this section, each of the FLICS categories will be discussed and skill-session activities designed for practicing certain verbal behaviors will be presented. You can do some of these skill sessions alone as you read, but all of them are more effective when done in small groups, to allow for discussion and cross-fertilization of ideas.

Teacher Talk

(1) *Accepts Feeling:* The teacher uses this category when he acknowledges through reflection, clarification, or identifica-

tion existence of pupil feelings that have been expressed explicitly or implicitly.

This category is nonjudgmental, as opposed to the categories of praise and criticism, which definitely tell pupils that their behavior is good or bad, right or wrong. Table 1 gives examples of acceptance through reflection ("You feel upset"), clarification ("you feel angry because you believe you were unfairly treated"), and identification ("I understand how you feel" and "People often cry when they are hurt."). *Reflection* can be mere repetition, but since this often sounds rather stilted, it is better to use synonyms where possible. That is, if a child says, "I hate science and I'm not going to do it," rather than accepting his statement by saying, "You hate science and you're not going to do it," which is exact repetition, it is more helpful to say, "I guess you're kind of upset about the science assignment today." *Clarification* implies some interpretation and might be used to help youngsters determine what is upsetting them. "We're feeling kind of restless because it's so hot in here." "I know we don't feel much like going on with our work after all that excitement." "No wonder you're so upset; that was really a frightening experience." "You're mad at me because I insisted that you move your seat earlier." *Identification* can refer to either personal identification, "I know how you must feel," or to general identification, "Not everyone likes everybody else all of the time." Feelings accepted can be positive ones as well as negative ones: "You really feel good about that!" "No wonder you're so happy, that was a marvelous performance," or "I know how really great you must feel." If you start your sentences with "You feel," "I guess you feel," "You seem to feel . . ." this will help you come up with a (1).

Acceptance of feeling is not widely found in classrooms, or, for that matter, in life in general. Since most of us do not hear this verbal behavior very often, we particularly need to practice it if we wish to acquire it. Remember, whether or not you use any behavior is a matter you must decide for yourself, but if you do not own certain behaviors then you cannot even make the choice of whether or not to use them. So it is wise to acquire *many* behaviors in order to be able to call forth from a wide repertory when the need arises. Knowing how to accept feelings is particularly valuable for giving support to persons who need a sympathetic ear, because it can encourage people to talk and explore their feelings. It's also useful for cutting hostility and for beginning to work on changing behavior. For example, many teachers would criticize the child who says, "I hate Jimmy!" in a number of ways; saying things like, "Who do you think you are saying that in this classroom! Don't you ever let me hear that kind of talk again!" (7ah) or, "Now, you know you don't really feel that way. In this classroom we all like each other." (7a) The first teacher comment will not make the child feel less angry toward Jimmy, and he will undoubtedly feel hostile toward the teacher as well. The teacher may suppress the *expression* of the anger—while he is watching, at least, but does nothing to help deal with the feelings. The second comment simply denies the existence of the feelings and says that kind of feeling (dislike) doesn't exist. While not arousing the hostility of the first and harsher statement, the second does nothing constructive to deal with the feelings.

Examples of the use of acceptance of feeling directed to the statement "I hate Jimmy" would be "I guess you're pretty mad at Jimmy right now," or "Everybody gets mad at other people sometimes." Note how different acceptance is from praise. Praise would be completely inappropriate: "It's good that you don't like Jimmy." Acceptance of feeling isn't *always* appropriate when feelings are expressed, nor is it the only possible helpful behavior. One might ask a question after a child says he hates another: "What seems to be the problem between you?" Often, however, the teacher needs only to recognize and accept feelings in order to bring about desired behavior. If a child says, "I don't want to clean up!" and the teacher says, "It is kind of a pain to have to clean up, I know," this may be enough to cure the problem. With no further ado the child will begin cleaning up.

Feelings that are expressed in nonverbal ways can be accepted also—grimaces, smiles, fidgeting, tears, and so on. "You seem to be mad (or happy) today." "It's okay to cry—you're really upset, I know!" Feelings past or future can be accepted as well as present ones. For example, if a class has had a great deal of difficulty with a certain concept or lesson, the teacher might start the new lesson by saying, "Yesterday we had a lot of trouble with this and we were quite upset about it (1) so today let's see where the problems are and see if we can't straighten things out." (5) An example of acknowledging a probable future feeling is, "Some of you might get worried tomorrow when the tests are passed out, and that's a very natural and common feeling at test time."

Skill Session I: Acceptance of Feeling

Divide into groups of three or four, and together write down teacher acceptances to the following pupil behaviors or statements using more than one means, if possible (reflection, clarification, identification).

1. "I really hate science and I don't see why we even have it."
2. "I don't like my baby brother."
3. A child spends most of the period daydreaming.
4. "What does that old art teacher have to always be coming here for."
5. "Boy that game was fun."
6. A child is hesitant about entering any group during free activity time.
7. "Who wants to be on a committee with him!"
8. "I like you."
9. "You're an old witch and I wish I wasn't in your class!"
10. "Nobody likes me."
11. A child is smiling while reading a story to himself.
12. "I wish I wasn't so bad all the time."
13. "It makes me mad when that teacher tells us we don't do good work."
14. "Who cares what you say!"

15. A child looks puzzled and upset while reading directions.
16. "Why do we have to go to those awful assembly programs all the time!"
17. "Ow! I hurt my knee." (Child is crying.)
18. A child makes an angry face at the teacher.
19. "I'm not going to be any good in our panel discussion."
20. "You can just go to hell!"

Do the same with these statements of teachers or future teachers:

1. "I believe that it's silly and a waste of time to accept pupils' impolite words or behaviors."
2. "I don't see any point in this assignment."
3. "The kids in my class are so impossible that nobody could do a good job with them."
4. "Well, if I ever had any decent courses, maybe I would have had a chance to learn to handle kids with these kinds of problems."
5. "I don't think I'm any good at teaching math."
6. "Maybe I shouldn't be a teacher."
7. "I'm worried about tomorrow's test."
8. "I just don't seem to understand what's going on."
9. "The principal there is simply impossible to deal with."
10. "My co-workers are totally uninterested in the children."
11. "I really love what I'm doing."
12. "My lesson today was really great."
13. "Some of the kids I have are so cute."
14. "This whole program is really a waste of time."
15. "I don't think I'll ever be able to control the kids."
16. "My project is absolutely lousy."
17. "Some people in the class always hog the discussion."

18. "If you'd ever stop talking, maybe someone else would have a chance."
19. "That kid is so horrible and so disruptive that no one could handle him."
20. "What's the use of killing myself—nobody in that school gives a damn."

Skill Session II: Acceptance of Feeling

If you are teaching, think of examples from recent days when you might have accepted feeling, or did accept feeling, and discuss these in your group.

(2) _Praise:_ In this category the teacher praises pupil behavior by (a) giving no reason or personal approval without any further explanation or (b) by giving an explanation, called a rational reason, as to why the praise is given.

Praising without reasons ("right" "good") or with just the reason that the teacher approves ("I like that behavior,") is common classroom behavior. Any visitor to a classroom will hear teacher talk that would fall under the 2a category: "That's good work," "Right," "Nice report," "That's a lovely picture," "You're sitting well," "You walked through the halls nicely," "I'm proud of your work," "Correct." However, the visitor is less likely to hear reasons given for praise, the behavior which we tally as 2b. We will concentrate on this behavior since it is less common, and its acquisition needs some practice. We know that one way children learn to reason is to hear reasons given (and, of course, to _personally_ engage in reasoning). In addition to using rational reasons in order to help the reasoning ability of pupils, giving explicit reasons for praise helps everyone understand why certain ideas or behaviors _are_ praiseworthy. For example, if a child gives a report to the class and the teacher says afterwards, "Nice work," there is no specific information about why the report was good. But if a teacher says, "Using graphs as you did to show population growth and other statistics was a good idea, because that helped us quickly see changes and relations," or, "You looked at us when you spoke, which was good because it helped us to feel more involved," the reporter gets useful feedback, and, in addition, everyone hears reasons, and can make use of the information in his own work.

Teachers will, of course, continue to use praise with personal reasons and no reasons, and that is to be expected. The point is to use rational reasons at particularly helpful times, and we need to *learn* to include the 2b's in our talk. If you find yourself frequently saying "*I* am proud of you," "*I* like your behavior," "*I*," "*I*," "*I*," then you may need to clarify your feelings toward dependency. Presumably we want youngsters to walk quietly through the halls in order not to disturb other people, not merely to make *us* proud of them. This is not to say that as teachers we should never say things like "I'm proud of you"—only that, as in all the suggestions offered in this book, we need to examine our behavior so that our choices are made rationally according to desired goals.

The inclusion of "I" doesn't always make the statement a 2a—for example, "I think your idea is helpful because it incorporates both points of view and would get us out of this impasse," has an "*I* think" included, but gives rational reasons for the helpfulness of the idea. In all the talk categories, tone of voice is important. A teacher may say, "I see that you handed in your unusual marvelous looking paper," in a sarcastic tone of voice to a child whose work is messy, and the meaning is "this paper is awful." This teacher comment would be counted as a 7, criticism, not a 2.

In both the following examples youngsters have given reports and the whole class is commenting in "good" ways. That is, they have been encouraged to be helpful to the person giving the report.

These are the comments from pupils in one situation: "It was good." "You shouldn't have it so long." "I don't think it was too long." "Well I did." "It was interesting." "Yeah it was good." "The part about what might happen later was good."

The second situation elicits these comments from pupils:

"Well, I thought the way you looked around at the class was good—instead of looking only at your paper." "I liked that you asked us to write down three reasons why we thought books might not be used in the future—because then I was more interested in what you would say." "Maybe you could have had some pictures of the early books you talked about—the scrolls and clay tablets—then we would have known more what they were." "I liked the part about on a desert island would you rather have some books, some pencils and paper, or a working TV set. That made me know what I thought about books compared to the others."

We can see the difference in these two examples between using praise and criticism with and without reasons. The pupils in the first situation said little that would indicate precisely what was "good" or "bad" about the report, while the pupils in the second situation gave useful specific reasons for their comments to the reporter.

Here are some additional examples of praise with rational reasons:

1. "That's an interesting collage because you folded the paper in such unusual ways before you pasted it on the big paper."
2. "Good, you're remembering to keep your eye on the ball as you hit it."
3. "Fine, you held the door for the people behind you."
4. "You people were so wonderfully quiet going through the hall that you wouldn't have disturbed even the shyest mouse!"
5. "Your ending on this story is particularly good, because it's what could logically have happened, even though the whole thing is a fantasy."
6. Inviting both the second grade and the fifth grade is a really good idea because then we'll know how younger children and older children respond to our program.
7. "How nice! You used blocks in all kinds of ways to

connect different parts of the buildings, so the people and cars can get from one place to another very easily."

8. "Your picture is particularly pleasing because you used all those bright colors and then added the touch of black as a contrast."

9. "That's right, because an ounce is less than a pound so the boy with the ounce of candy had less to share."

Skill Session III: Praise

Divide into groups of three or four and change the following examples of praise given with personal reasons or no reasons to praise with rational reasons. Write down your changes (usually a "because" would be added after each statement). Be sure to be *specific*—avoid statements like, "Your reading is improving because you read that whole page."

1. "Your idea about taking a trip is a good one."
2. "Your book report is excellent."
3. "Your paper on life in hot, dry lands is good."
4. "I like the way you're sitting."
5. "That's the right way to hold the pencil."
6. "You played the softball game well."
7. "Your behavior on the trip was terrific."
8. "Your work on that committee was helpful."
9. "What good penmanship."
10. "That's a fine question for this unit on transportation."
11. "Your division example is correct."
12. "Your suggestions for the party is a good one."
13. "Your hair looks nice today."
14. "This is a good essay on schools."
15. "Your conduct in the assembly was excellent."
16. "That's a fine block building."
17. "You're working very well together at the puzzle table.

18. "You were good cleaners today."
19. "Your reading is improving."
20. "You got into groups nicely today."
21. "That's a good suggestion for a name for a new country."
22. "That's a good idea for a science project to show first graders."
23. "You sang well today."

Skill Session IV: Praise

Think of examples from your own teaching, when you might have given rational reasons for praise and discuss these in your group.

(3) *Acceptance of Ideas:* Teachers use this category when they repeat, acknowledge, summarize, clarify, or develop ideas put forth by pupils. This category, like category (1), the acceptance of feelings, is nonjudgmental—the ideas accepted are not necessarily judged in terms of right or wrong. *Repetition* is exactly that; a pupil says, "I think we should go to Washington on our class trip," and the teacher says, "You think we should go to Washington." *Acknowledging* can be a nonjudgmental "okay" or "all right." (However, when these are said in the tone of voice which is the equivalent of "good" or "right!" these should be counted as 2's.) "That's one idea," "There's another idea," and "Jane thinks we should visit the country's capital" are also examples of acknowledgment. An example of *summarizing* is given in this teacher statement which occurs after several persons have spoken. "So far we've heard a number of suggestions: that we visit Washington; that we go to New York; that we don't go anywhere and use the money for a worthwhile cause like a scholarship; that we get to know our own group better by camping together for a few days; and, oh yes, that we visit the Pennsylvania Dutch country." An example of *clarification* would be the teacher saying, after some pupils say,

"We aren't even talking about the topic! We said we'd talk about where to take our trip," "Some new ideas are coming out here which we haven't heard before—some for unusual kinds of trips and some which aren't trips at all. This is making the discussion somewhat different from what we'd planned." *Development* is used in this example: "Several people have suggested that we go camping for a few days, evidently because they believe the most important kind of trip we could take would be one that would bring us closer together—one where we'd live and work together in the outdoors rather than go sightseeing."

The important difference between praise and acceptance is that praise specifically indicates that ideas or behaviors are correct, or good. Acceptance, on the other hand, *acknowledges* the ideas. While acceptance may indicate that contributions are of value to the group ("that's another idea"), when we use this category we do not say "right" or "good." One can even accept wrong answers, for example, when the teacher asks, "Why is it that some people are taller than others?" "Because they're stronger and they eat more," responds one pupil. "You think some people are taller because they eat more," the teacher accepts this idea by repeating it. "I think it's because they're older," says another pupil. "Well I'm not as old as my cousin and I'm tall," someone else joins in. "You think some people are taller because they're older, but Ken says that's not always so," accepts the teacher. "Fathers are taller than mothers," comes from another pupil. "All right," acknowledges the teacher. "Some people smoke, so they don't get so tall," says one child. "There's another idea," is another teacher acknowledgment. "I'm going to be tall when I grow up," "Me too," "Everyone will be taller when they grow up," "I think some people are taller because they do exercise," are other reasons put forth by children. "Now we have still more ideas," says the teacher.

In the preceding situation the teacher asked the youngsters to hypothesize when she asked, "Why is it that some people are taller than others?" and she didn't want to say "right" and "wrong" after anyone's contribution. She wanted to get out the youngsters' hunches and do some verifying later. And if you want to get out hunches, it will not usually be helpful to say judgmental things like "You're really thinking!" "That's not sensible," "That's good," or "I don't think that's quite it" because then some children will be hesitant to try. You will have more of a creative brainstorming atmosphere if you can learn to accept ideas without judging them.

Skill Session V: Acceptance of Ideas

In small groups, role play a conversation in which the teacher asks the following questions and then *cannot* praise. The person playing the role of teacher must accept all responses. He can also ask questions or give information if this is appropriate. For some of these role plays (depending on the topic) be yourselves, for others role play the part of younger pupils.

1. "Some people say that books are going to be outdated in a few years—that we won't use them anymore. Why do you think this is being said?"
2. "What do you think about making free college education available to everyone—whatever his high school record may have been?"
3. "Why do you think we eat different kinds of foods instead of just deciding on two or three that we like best and sticking to those?"
4. "What other ways could we have for learning if all schools as we know them would have to be closed forever, starting tomorrow?"
5. "What can we do in this class so that things will be less noisy and more people will pay attention?"
6. "Many people believe grades are of no value and are actually harmful. What do you think about that?"

Change these underlined statements of praise to statements of acceptance of ideas. Change them in more than one way, using repetition, acknowledgment, summary, clarification, and development. Work in small groups and actually write down your statements.

1. "The man could have found his way home by asking somebody." "<u>Good</u>."
2. "The boys and girls who lived then didn't have much fun." "<u>That's right</u>."
3. "A long time ago people used to have to make most of their things, or grow them and things like that, because there was hardly any stores to go to." "<u>Right</u>."
4. "If you look down the whole column of numbers before you add, and pick out the things that add up to tens and fives, you could add faster." "<u>Good thinking</u>."
5. "If people don't get along together, then they should try to talk about the trouble, or get somebody else to talk with them, or they should not do things together." "<u>That's good thinking</u>!"
6. "A dictionary is a place where you could find words." "<u>Correct</u>."
7. "The reason why cities often grew up around rivers or on seacoasts is because the people had a way to get there and also the supplies had a way to get there." "<u>Fine</u>."
8. "If we gave ourselves grades we'd all get A's, so what's the point?" "<u>You're really thinking</u>!"
9. "If there weren't any mirrors or any other things that we could see ourselves in, well we wouldn't know what we look like and we wouldn't fix ourselves up, so we'd look terrible—or maybe other people would comb our hair and stuff like that." "<u>Good point</u>."
10. "I don't think that negative feelings should be accepted or acknowledged. I believe that if a child tells a teacher he doesn't like her, he needs to be taught a few manners!" "<u>That's a good point</u>."

11. "I don't think we should have wars because what's the use anyway. All that happens is that people get killed —and the wars didn't make that much difference anyway. Look at us and Canada. We had a war with England, and they didn't and what's the difference between us?" "Good thinking."
12. "The reason the Indians had different kinds of houses is because sometimes they lived near where there was trees, but sometimes they didn't so they had to use something else like skins." "Very good."

Skill Session VI: Acceptance of Ideas

If you are teaching, think of the times when you might have accepted ideas, rather than praised or criticized, and discuss these in your groups.

(4) *Asking Questions:* The next chapter will be devoted to the study and practice of asking questions, and therefore will not be dealt with here.

(5) *Giving Information or Opinion:* When using this category the teacher tells his own ideas or opinions, or presents content from other sources, or offers explanations to the pupils. Rhetorical questions also fit into this category. ("Why did the president issue that particular document at that time? Well, he did so because . . .") Fives can be a few words long, or they can be extended lectures.

The words "yes" or "no" can be 5's if they are used to give information. If a child says, "Did you think that was a good program?" The answer of "yes" or "no" will be counted as a 5. This is quite different from the "yes" or "no" that means "right" or "wrong."

Many teachers begin lessons with category 5—they present information or opinion. Then they ask questions about what they have just presented, which generally means that they ask recall questions only. However, if teachers begin lessons or activities by involving children, for example, through encouraging them to hypothesize, to tell what they know and don't know about the material at hand, this helps the pupils become more interested in the information which is to follow and also involves them in higher levels of thought than that involved in simply listening to some input and then retrieving what they have heard.

Let's think of a spelling lesson in which a teacher begins by telling the children the spelling rule " 'i' before 'e' except after 'c,' or when sounded like 'a' as in 'neighbor' or 'weigh.' " The children learn the rule and then apply it through recall— they have had little opportunity for thought. Another teacher might say, "Let's see if we can figure out how to decide whether to put 'i' or 'e' first in words that have those two letters together. How could we do that?" and go on to have the children build lists of words spelled both ways, trying to arrive at the generalization themselves concerning the rule about "i" before "e." In this latter instance the children engage in a higher level of thinking activity than they do by memorizing the rule.

Another example of activity involving the class, using adults this time, would be for an instructor to ask the class to think about what teachers do when they teach, then move into building a list of the kinds of talk that teachers use in classrooms and then introduce some information about existing category systems. This would be more involving than giving a lecture presentation about category systems for analyzing classroom talk, without involving the class in any other way than as listeners. The instructor would feed in information in both these instances, but the information would very likely be better received, remembered, and applied in the first instance.

I am continuously struck by the lack of implementation of interesting teaching methods among educators. Most staff meetings on the school or college level are boring partly because little effort is made to involve the participants, and communication tends to be one-way lecture presentations of matters which could have been handled in writing. When teachers are involved in giving presentations to peers, it is usually necessary to review method of presentation with them and concentrate strongly on how this can be done in creative and involving ways. Otherwise they will give reports which they read, or they will have a panel of speakers. This is a serious indictment of the means we are using for teaching about the importance of method. Most "methods courses" fail on two counts: they present content rather than method, and the methods used within the course do not serve as models for teachers. We act as if the message were all that mattered, yet we are surrounded by evidence telling us that the message is often lost because of the way in which it is presented.

Skill Session VII: Giving Information or Opinion

Divide into small groups of from four to six persons and plan some sort of presentation to the class, in which you will be giving information but in which you will involve the class members in a variety of ways you believe will interest them. Decide upon any relevant topic and then actually plan an hour presentation—whether or not you carry it through. You need not merely use category 5 for your presentation.

(6) *Gives Direction:* Teachers use this behavior when they tell students to take certain specific actions, when they give commands of either an instructional or managerial nature. This can be done calmly or harshly (indicated by an "h"), and it is tone of voice which is the primary differentiating factor here. For example, "Sit down now" said calmly has a quite different feeling tone from "Sit down now!" screamed at the class or at one or a few children. Pupils feel quite differently about these two deliveries.

Many teachers have a tendency to give directions and then criticize those pupils who aren't following them, and then give further directions and follow this with more criticism. Flanders refers to this behavior as "the vicious circle" or "the 6–7 trap." An example of this behavior follows.

Classroom A

"All right now, clear your desks. It's time for math. I said clear your desks! What are you two talking about—didn't you hear what I said! Get those desks cleared! Billy, you still aren't ready, now hurry up! All right, now take out your math workbooks. You two are *still* talking, and if you don't stop you're going to find yourself down in the office! And look at this row— half of you still don't have your desks cleared. Now *get out those workbooks*! All right, open to page 24. I see, Billy, that you still don't know how to read numbers—and *what* are you doing back there! This class can never do anything properly!"

The preceding teaching behavior is inefficient because the pupils do not improve in following the teachers directions, even though he gives more and more of them and continues to critisize the pupils for not complying. We soon know which children have difficulty in clearing desks, getting work out, and so on, and we can help them by giving some warning a few minutes beforehand, so that they have an idea of how much longer they have to work. In addition, moving about the room and helping those children who are perpetually slow at moving on to the next activity and encouraging youngsters to help each other clear desks and find correct page numbers is efficient teaching behavior. Also, effective teachers will reward that behavior which is acceptable rather than constantly criticizing what is wrong. An example of this kind of teaching follows.

Classroom B

"All right now, the five minutes is up. Are we ready for math? Let's see if we can get our desks cleared, with our math books out, so we'll be all set. Don, let's get all these crayons into this box. Jane, can you help Jimmy clear his desk—he has so much stuff out, I think he'll appreciate a little aid there. And Vinny, I see that you have everything put away already. I think that must be some kind of a record. This whole table over here is all set. Great! That's really fast work. Fine, I think everybody is ready—now let's open to page 24. I'm going to put the number up here on the board so we all know what it looks like, and

I'll walk around and you show me by having the book open on your desk that you know where the place is. You can ask your neighbor to help you find it if you like. Okay, everyone has the number, and we're ready to go."

In the second situation the teacher personally helped pupils and encouraged them to help each other, and she praised those who followed directions rather than criticizing those who did not—her purpose wasn't to "get the kids." It is important, always, to think about what it is you really want to teach. Do you want to teach youngsters that adults (in particular, you) are scolding, critical people who are extremely difficult to please and who operate on the principle of might makes right? Or do you want them to learn that you as an adult/teacher are a helpful person, there to assist them in learning and to encourage them to help each other rather than to compete with each other and disregard others' welfare. One reason many of us are so directive and critical is that we ourselves have been so frequently directed and criticized from infancy on. If we want youngsters to be accepting, helpful people, we need to model these behaviors for them.

(7) *Criticizing or Rejecting Ideas, Feelings, Behavior:* When using this category the teacher criticizes or rejects by (a) giving no reasons or expressing personal disapproval without further explanation or by (b) giving a rational explanation about why the criticism is being expressed. There is an ("h") for "harshly," because there seems to be an important difference in effect between the response of a calmly spoken "That's not right" to the pupil statement "2 and 2 is 5," and a vindictive "Can't you get even the simplest kind of example right?" Notice that though the last statement is in question form, it is not counted as such because no answer is expected, and it is so clearly critical.

The previous discussion of reasons for giving praise holds for this category as well. Once again, it is important to practice giving reasons, at least some of the time, so that you will not always say, "No," "Wrong," or "I don't like that behavior."

Examples A

1. "That's not what I told you to do!"
2. "Is that the way to hold your pencil!"
3. "What are you two doing!"
4. "Just exactly who told you to do things that way?"
5. "That's not the way to fold the paper!"
6. "As usual you're doing everything wrong!"
7. "Don't hold your arm that way!"

Teachers could say, with little change in the number of words used, but much change in the amount of help offered:

Examples B

1. "I asked you to put three lines on the left side."
2. "If you hold your pencil a little higher up, I think you'll be able to write more easily."
3. "You two need to put that game away now and join the rest of us."
4. "Put the numbers to be added directly under each other on the page."
5. "Fold your paper so that you end up with a triangle."
6. "I think you need to go back a bit. Begin here, and check with June to see how she did it."
7. "Hold your arm in a graceful curve over your head."

In Examples A, the teacher criticizes in ways that are not really helpful, that merely convey annoyance. In Examples B, the teacher explains what ought to be done, or offers helpful comments in some way—either through giving clear directions or through giving information. When we feel annoyed it is often hard not to criticize pupils, but if we think about what we really want to accomplish, this will help us to shelve our annoyance

"Why do you keep on being the same way, when I've told you over and over what you're like?"

Drawing by Saxon; © 1958 The New Yorker Magazine, Inc.

and speak so that we assist pupils rather than vent our own anger. While in some instances releasing anger is both honest and helpful (telling the pupils "I'm *really* angry now, and I feel extremely annoyed at all of you,"), at other times criticism merely makes youngsters hostile and sets up a kind of cycle of anger between you and them—or makes the children uneasy and unsure of themselves and frightened of both you and the subject matter. If we remember that our job is to teach, and then think about what sort of teaching *we* prefer, helpful assistance or hostile reprimands, we may be better able to keep our cool with the children and tell them in helpful ways what is expected. So—some of the time you may want to criticize behavior with reasons; at other times you may want to omit criticism entirely. It's important at times to just say what to do rather than waste time on any form of criticism.

Remember, too, when dealing with ideas, the importance of staying with the child whose answer is wrong, either directly to give him the right answer and explain why his response is wrong or to help him to achieve the right answer. Many teachers simply ask a question and then call on pupils until they find someone to whom they can say "Right" without checking to find out why the wrong answers were given and whether the youngsters who gave the wrong answers now understand the reasons behind the correct answer.

Skill Session VIII: Criticizing and Rejecting Ideas, Feelings, and Behavior

Change these criticisms without reasons either to criticism with reasons or to another category that contains no criticism. You might, for instance, accept what's logical and give corrective feedback. See number 15 for an example of this.

1. "Stop doing that with your chair."
2. "Don't hold the book that way."
3. "You mean you didn't even know the sun is a star!"
4. "That's not the way to write this addition example."

5. "I didn't say to use those colors."
6. "You don't have the words right in that song."
7. "That word is not 'when.' "
8. "Just because it's snowing today does *not* mean it's winter!"
9. "Look at the dirt on your hands!"
10. "Don't your shoelaces ever stay tied?"
11. "Why can't you ever do anything right?"
12. "As usual, you aren't ready."
13. "If you'd pay attention, you'd know where your place was supposed to be in the book."
14. "4 plus 5 is not 8!"
15. "New York City is not the capital of New York state." *Corrective feedback without rejection.* (We often think that the capital of the state is the largest and best-known city—as New York City is. Why don't you come up here to the map and check out your answer?)
16. "Don't call me names, young man!"
17. "Don't cry about it!"
18. "A rectangle and a square are not the same thing."
19. "Don't say 'ain't.' "
20. "Don't slam your books down, young lady! Who do you think you are?"

Skill Session IX

If you are working with children, think of times recently when you might have given reasons for criticism; or given corrective feedback without criticism, and discuss these with your group.

Pupil Talk

(8) *Responds to Teacher:* This category of pupil talk indicates speech which is in response to solicitation from the teacher.

Even if an answer is wrong, it is counted as an 8. If the teacher asks, "How much is 2 and 2?" and the pupils says, "5," that answer is counted as category 8—response to teacher. However, if the teacher asks, "How much is 2 and 2?" and the pupil says, "You said we could have art today," or, "Yesterday I counted up to 50," or "If you put two 2's together, that's 22," then these are not counted as 8's but as 9's—pupil initiations to the teacher. No matter how broad or narrow the question, called-for responses to questions are counted as 8's.

(9) *Pupil Initiates Talk to Teacher:* This category is used when pupils initiate talk to the teacher without the teacher's solicitation. If the teacher asks a question and the child doesn't directly respond, but brings up something new, that is a 9. When pupils initiate topics of their own and direct these to the teacher, for example, "Shall we wear our coats outside today," "Where shall I write my name?" "I think you look nice today," "Why don't we all decide together what we want to study instead of just you deciding," "Why does he always get to go on errands?", "You spelled that word wrong," these are 9's.

(10) *Pupil Talk to Total Class or Individual Pupils:* This category is reserved for pupil talk that is directed to the class, including the teacher, as opposed to talk directed only to the teacher or primarily to the teacher. It is reserved for true group discussion, or for genuine interaction between two or more pupils.

In order to achieve this kind of discussion, teachers have to do specific things, for example, have the children work in small groups or arrange the seats so that they face *each other* rather than the front of the room and each others' backs. The teacher may have to directly remind pupils—often—to speak to each other, to look at each other, to tell each other what they think and feel. Certainly the teacher will have to refrain from speaking to each person's point if he wants them to move away from speaking only to him, although he might need to speak between contributions by saying, "What do the rest of you think?", "Would anyone like to add to that?", "Does everyone agree?", "Who disagrees?" and so on. Teachers may want to set a rule that they won't talk until two or three pupils have spoken, and share this rule with the class, telling them why. These suggestions will help to achieve 10's in the classroom.

(11) *Silence:* This category indicates silence *during periods of conversation.* That is, if you were tallying classroom behavior and the class began to read silently, or do quiet seatwork, then you would stop tallying—there would be no point in listing lines of 11's. At the beginning of this chapter, in the discussion of the college classroom situation, it was mentioned that when a teacher asks a thought-provoking question, he ought to give the pupils time to think. For many reasons teachers tend to fill in a silence after a question in a number of ways. They may rephrase the question, usually making it more narrow, they may ask a different question, they may answer the question, they may call on someone, they may criticize the class for not responding. In order to allow for silence after questions, most people need to train themselves to wait. Nothing very terrible will happen if one does wait, and one always has the same options to use somewhat later if no one answers even after being given plenty of thought time.

(Z) *Confusion:* This is a category which indicates that there is so much noise going on that the lesson cannot be followed. You can put Z's next to other numbers when you are actually tallying classroom behavior, if you can follow the lesson, even though there is considerable noise. If discussion groups were meeting, the noise resulting from this would not be counted as Z's, unless the assigned work was not being done and there was aimless noise. When you are tallying and the class goes into small group work you can either stop tallying or you can sit in one group and observe their behavior, using teacher categories for group members, if the teacher is not actually a member of that group.

We have now gone through the FLICS, with the exception of the question categories, which will be covered in the next chapter. The FLICS is meant to help you broaden your talk repertory and consciously select talk according to what will be most productive. This is not easy, because one of the difficulties in teaching is that decisions have to be made continuously and rapidly, which means that teachers need to make instant talk decisions in many different situations with many different children. You will need to know when, and with whom, to use which kinds of talk, but having a wide repertory to draw upon is an important first step.

The FLICS and the Teacher's Goals

The FLICS is to be used as a self-evaluative instrument, whether it is used by the teacher himself, analyzing a tape of his teaching, or with the aid of a supervisor. This category system is designed to help teachers and student teachers change in ways in which *they* want to change, according to the goals they have set. People must *want* to modify their behavior before they become open to change, and pleasing a supervisor is not usually a strong enough reason for continued behavior change. If the supervisor makes suggestions with which the teacher does not agree, then it is likely that changed behavior will occur while the supervisor watches, but not when the teacher is alone. One assumption underlying the use of self-evaluative instruments is that people want to improve their teaching and will do so when given help and support.

Because the teacher's own goals are important, it is essential to look at the FLICS in the light of those goals. For example, if a teacher wants to involve students in group discussion and wants to accept their contributions in a certain lesson, but finds when listening to the playback of a tape or when looking at the tallies of his teaching made by an observer that the behavior shows:

4—question
8—response
5—lecture

4—question
8—response
4—question
8—response
2—praise
4—question
8—response
7—criticism

then the teacher would not be satisfied that he had achieved his goal—which would have called for (10's) pupil talk to the total class and (3's) acceptance of ideas by the teacher. However, if the teacher were conducting a math drill and the pattern was:

4a—recall question
8—response
2a—praise
4a—recall question
8—response
2a—praise

then he would be satisfied with these results. So the FLICS *must* be used in reference to the goals of the teacher, *by* the teacher; and if behavior change is to occur, that must be change the teacher *wants* to achieve.

When the FLICS or other observation instruments are used by supervisors with teachers or student teachers, it is important for supervisors to be aware of their own talk. If supervisors use recall questions, praise and criticism without reasons, lecture, and directions in their own talk during the supervisory conference to tell teachers to use more acceptance of feeling and ideas, more praise and criticism with reasons, and varied questions which call for productive responses, then they will miss the opportunity to serve as models of the behavior they are trying to encourage. This is, of course, true for college instructors in their courses as well. Flanders has formulated the rule of two thirds, which says that in the average classroom someone is talking two thirds of the time, two thirds of *that* time the teacher is doing the talking, and two thirds of the average teacher's talk is lecture, direction-giving, and criticism. Since educators seem to agree that more productive learning takes place if pupils talk more, and if teachers' talk is accepting and encouraging and contains questions that go beyond recall and retrieval, then everyone in education should become more conscious of his talk and strive for change—away from Flanders' rule of two thirds.

The FLICS can be introduced to pupils in the classroom, although if the children are in the primary grades you should probably simplify the system by leaving out some of the sub-categories and change the language if it is too technical. You can put the system on a chart and let youngsters refer to it during the day. This is a good way for teachers and pupils to become more conscious of their behavior and to give each other feedback. However, if a child says, "You used a lot of 7's," then it will not be helpful to respond with, "No wonder—if you'd behave better, I wouldn't have to do that!" Be willing to listen to children, and try a response like, "I guess you think I'm too critical," or, "Perhaps I do—what could I have said instead of what I did?" This latter reply is, of course, a question, and it is to questions that we shall now turn our attention.

Selected References

Edmund Amidon and Elizabeth Hunter. *Improving Teaching: The Analysis of Classroom Verbal Interaction*, New York: Holt, Rinehart and Winston, Inc., 1966.

Ned Flanders. *Analyzing Teaching Behavior*, Reading, Mass.: Addison-Wesley Publishing Company, Inc., 1970.

5

who? what? where? when?
—and more important, how? why?
classroom questions

Asking questions is one of the most common of all teaching strategies. However, most teachers have had little training in formulating questions or in building questions in any sequential or hierarchical order. Most of us have not had many opportunities to respond to productive and provocative questions as pupils, and we have had even fewer opportunities to ask good questions as school youngsters. For many of us the ability to ask those "hows" and "why" of early childhood days has been blunted rather than sharpened by schooling. Since the level of thinking engaged in depends upon the level of questions asked, and since most teachers ask recall questions most of the time, this means that retrieval or rote-memory thinking is what is usually expected of pupils—"whos," "whats," "wheres," and "whens." My experience indicates, however, that teachers are eager to ask the more productive questions—the "hows" and "whys"—but that they need practice and guidance. This chapter provides some of the necessary tools for generating productive classroom questions.

One caution must be kept in mind about classroom questions. Many educators have pointed out that in most classrooms it is neither the question nor the answer that is particularly important to the pupils, who are primarily concerned with being "right" in the eyes of the teacher. That is, thinking is not really what matters to most youngsters; what counts is pleasing the person in charge—the teacher. If you want to upgrade the cognitive level of your classroom, and questions are of prime importance in cognition, then you must always be sensitive to the affective climate as well. If *your* way is the only acceptable way and you are training children, either consciously or unconsciously, to "psych you out," then productive thinking will certainly be stifled in your classroom.

The FLICS Category 4—Asking Questions

The five subcategories of questions included under category 4 of the FLICS are taken from the work of Guilford[1] as developed by Gallagher and Aschner.[2]

The teacher *asks questions*, which involve:

(a) Recall: involves facts and rote memory, is narrow. "What is the name of the game we played yesterday?"

[1] J. P. Guilford, "The Structure of Intellect," *Psychological Bulletin,* Vol. 53 (1956), pp. 267–293.

[2] James M. Gallagher and Mary Jane Aschner, "A Preliminary Report on Analyses of Classroom Interaction," *Merrill-Palmer Quarterly of Behavior and Development,* Vol. 9, pp. 183–194.

(b) Comprehension: calls for the processing of given or remembered data through analysis or integration. Answers can be right or wrong. "What are some differences between that game and dodge ball?"

(c) Invention: calls for answers that are creative and imaginative, that move in new directions. "What are some ways you could change this game so it would be more fun?" No one right answer.

(d) Evaluation: calls for judgment and choice. May be broad or narrow. "Do you like this game?" "What are some reasons why this might or might not be a good game?" "What are some reasons why this might or might not be a good game for adults and children to play together?" "Do you think games are as important as reading, and tell why."

(e) Routine: concerned with management. "Are we ready?" "Any questions?"

According to Gallagher and Aschner's definition, productive thinking includes those "operations whereby the individual draws upon available past and present acts, ideas, associations and observations in order to bring forth *new* facts, ideas and conclusions."[3] Therefore, the FLICS subcategory (a), recall, does not call for productive thinking because nothing new is expected; subcategories (b), (c), and (d) do, however, generate productive thinking. Subcategory (e), routine, is meant for questions that are concerned with classroom management rather than with thinking operations. We will concentrate our efforts, so far as practice is concerned, on the "whys" and "hows"; that is, on the categories of comprehension, invention, and evaluation.

Let's begin by looking at a number of examples of the four types of questions that deal with thinking as presented in the FLICS. Not all questions are spoken in question form. That is, when a teacher tells pupils to "compare" or "contrast," this may sound like a direction. However, even though there is no

[3] Gallagher and Aschner, p. 185.

question mark at the end of "Compare these two pictures," the statement is defined as a question—a comprehension question, because it calls for the processing of data through analysis.

Examples of FLICS Questions: [(a) is recall, (b) is comprehension, (c) is invention, (d) is evaluation].

1. a. What special holiday will occur this month?
   b. Contrast the way Thanksgiving is celebrated today with the way it was celebrated at the first Thanksgiving. Why do we have holidays?
   c. How would our lives be different if every day were a holiday? Invent a new national holiday and give the reasons for its existence and the means of celebration.
   d. Tell about your favorite holiday. What do you think about the decision to have certain holidays always occur on Mondays in order to provide three-day weekends?

2. a. What is the name of the story we read for today?
   b. Compare this story with the one we read yesterday. Why did the children in this story feel they had to run away from home? (This question is placed under comprehension because the story didn't explain why the children ran away. If this information were included in the story, the question would be recall.)
   c. Make up a new ending for this story. Make up two new endings for this story, one that's sad, and one that's happy. Invent a new character for this story and weave him in in some logical way.
   d. Tell about your favorite character in the story—and say why he's your favorite. If you could talk to the author of this story, what would you tell him that you think would help him make his next story more interesting? What did you think about the way he ended his story?

3. a. What is a synonym for the word "urban"?
   b. Compare the lives of an urban child and a rural child.
   c. Suppose a law were passed saying that people could not live together in cities any larger than 20,000 people, and towns had to be twenty miles distant from each other. How would you disperse the people and industries of New York state?
   d. In your judgment is there more advantage to growing up in a city or in a small town?

4. a. How much is 5 times 5?
   b. Compare the Roman and Arabic numeral systems and tell why we use Arabic numerals most of the time. Why do you think we spent so much time learning that other way of doing long division when now we actually do it this way, which is much shorter? (Note that this is not an evaluation question even though it says, "why do *you* think"!)
   c. Suppose numbers had not been invented. What would some of our problems be and how might we solve them?
   d. What do you think of the policy which exists in many tall buildings of not using the number 13 for any floor—that is, of skipping the numbering of floors from 12 to 14?

5. a. Is education a social science or a physical science?
   b. In what ways would an elementary school teacher need to be trained differently from a secondary school teacher? Why is it that many states are cutting down the number of education courses required of students although many students and teachers are saying they need *more* courses that will prepare them for teaching?
   c. Plan a new curriculum which would more effectively prepare teachers—either a curriculum for elemen-

tary school teachers, for secondary teachers, or for both.

d. What do you think of the many new proposals for moving teacher education programs more directly into schools and their surrounding communities?

6. a. Define the term "environment."

b. Why is there so much talk today about environmental or ecological problems?

c. Plan for life in the year 2000, deciding what goods and services are essential for reasonable standards of living for persons throughout the world which can actually be attained without the danger of ruining the earth.

d. Which do you regard as the most serious environmental problem and why did you choose what you did?

7. a. In what year did the Mayflower land?

b. Compare the lives of children in the Plymouth colony with your own lives. Why is it that the early settlers did not provide freedom of thought and worship to others, although they had come to this land so that they could worship as they liked?

c. How might this country be different today if all immigration had ceased after 1780? How would this country be different if the European settlers had been unable to kill or enslave other men?

d. Suppose you had twenty minutes to visit with the settlers in Plymouth colony. Knowing what you do, what five things would you tell them that you think would most help them improve their lives?

The seven preceding examples were intended to clarify for you the differences between the question subcategories. Remember, however, that the subcategory may change according to the age and status of the pupils. For example, the question,

"What is another way of doing this arithmetic example?" asked about a simple addition example would not call for divergent thinking in older children who know the various possibilities, but for young children who are just discovering new ways of combining numbers, the question *would* be divergent.

It is also important to remember that any question based on retrieval of what pupils have read or been told is a recall question. If the teacher tells the children on one day about the causes of the Civil War and the next day asks what these causes are, this is a recall question. When you are observing in classrooms, there are almost always clues in the talk that tell you whether lessons are review or are dealing with new material; therefore, making decisions about whether questions are productive or recall is not usually difficult.

Skill Session I—Labeling Questions

This skill session will give you practice in identifying question subcategories. *Decide whether each of the following questions is recall, comprehension, invention, or evaluation.* You can do this individually, in small groups, or as a total class.

1. What did you think of that story?
2. Who was Columbus?
3. What are some of the differences between these two men?
4. If you were given a choice, would you rather live today or 300 years from today?
5. How do you think our country would be different if the South had won the Civil War? (This is not an evaluation question merely because it includes the words "do you think." Only questions that ask a person to judge the ideas or opinions of others, to make choices, or to judge such things as stories, pictures, or objects are evaluation questions. A question like,

"Why do you think we usually put liquids in bottles rather than bowls?" is not really an "in your judgment" question, because there are specific reasons that cause us to put liquids in bottles; therefore this question is a comprehension question. "Why do you think your father goes to work?" is also comprehension, not evaluation; as is, "Why do you think doctors earn more than nurses or bus drivers?" Comprehension questions have right answers which are known. Divergent questions (which is what question number 5 is) call for answers that move in new directions, answers that are not necessarily known but that are based upon knowledge, and do not call primarily for the application of criteria. If question 5 were stated, "On what criteria do you think Smith based his statement that neither side won the Civil War?" then the question would be evaluative.)

6. Why are some television programs more popular with children than with adults?
7. If you could be in charge of a television station, what kinds of programs would you show?
8. How many windows are there in this room?
9. What are some new uses you can think of for this toy duck?
10. Why do you think people move about the earth? (Again—remember that "do you think" does not necessarily make a question evaluative.)
11. What would happen if all means of communication were cut off except for face-to-face talking?
12. Why do we fight with words sometimes and with our fists or with weapons at other times?
13. When, if ever, do you think people should hit each other?
14. Let's think of some new way of getting into groups, one we've never used before.

Skill Session II—Formulating Questions

Take the following recall questions and change them so that they become comprehension, then invention, and then evaluation questions. You may have to go somewhat far afield, and that's all right. It is not necessary to stay narrowly within the area. Remember in an earlier example when the recall question, "How much is 5 times 5?" was used, the evaluation question was, "What do you think of the policy in many tall buildings of not using the number 13 for any floors?"

1. Who was Columbus?
2. How many windows are there in this room?
3. What is the tallest mountain in the world?
4. What is the name of this tree?
5. What is one important element in water?
6. Who composed the opera *Madame Butterfly*?
7. Which person did I have to scold for making noise in the halls?
8. What did we say were some of the purposes of prehistoric art?
9. What is the dictionary definition for the word "volunteer"?
10. What is a noun?
11. What are the names of the two bones in the lower arm?
12. What is the name of the country we have been discussing today?
13. List the presidents in order of terms served.
14. Did the dog in this story go right home or did he go somewhere else first?
15. How many boys and girls are in this room?

Skill Session III—Modifying Questions from Current Content

1. If you are teaching, student teaching, tutoring, or participating in a school in any way, think of a recall question that you asked recently and formulate a comprehension, invention, and evaluation question within the same content area. Do this in pairs, if possible, each taking a turn. Then share your questions with at least one other couple; repeat the exercise, using different recall questions as starters each time.

2. Think of recall questions from courses you are currently taking and formulate comprehension, invention, and evaluation questions in the same content area, working in couples as described in example 1.

3. If you are teaching, take a recall question from each major area in your day's teaching and think of comprehension, invention, and evaluation questions for these areas. (Since most of us are not used to asking productive questions, and since this is difficult to do in the midst of all that goes on in a classroom during any given lesson, it is particularly important to write teaching questions down in advance.) Do this and then share your questions with other members, now or at the next class session.

4. Pretend that you are the instructor in one or more of the courses you are currently taking (including this one) and formulate productive questions for the class members. You can work in teams, if you wish, but be sure to share your results with other class members.

Skill Session IV—Role-Playing the FLICS Numbers

Now that you have some practice with the subcategories of questions in the FLICS, you should be familiar with the FLICS in its entirety. In this particular exercise, you will practice talking according to certain FLICS numbers. This is best done in trios, with one person playing the role of pupil, one being the teacher, and one acting as observer. The pupil can speak only 8's, 9's, and 10's, and the teacher will speak only the numbers 1 through 7.

You can talk for as long as you like on each number; however, *if* the number appears more than once in succession, then you *must* talk about three seconds for each time the number appears. That is, if you see an 8 followed by three 3's you will accept what the pupil has said for about nine seconds. One other instruction: look ahead so that both pupil and teacher speak logically. That is, if the numbers to be spoken are 4b, 8, 3, 3, 3, then the pupil must say something during his talk time that *can* be accepted for approximately nine seconds.

Here is an example of what this exercise entails:

TEACHER:
(1) "We seemed pretty upset and confused yesterday by the imperfect tense,
(5) so today I think it will be a good idea for us to go over the imperfect of *finir* once again and see where the trouble is."

PUPIL:
(9) "Well, I don't think I'll ever catch on, and I don't see why we have to know that tense anyway. The past, present, and future tenses are enough for us to know how to speak well."

TEACHER:
(1) "Well, I can understand your feelings about this being a difficult part of the language,
(7b) but you'll just have to try to learn it because it is on the standardized tests we have. We can't always do exactly as we like, or learn only what we want to learn, you know."
(6) "Now, open your books to page 102 and take a few moments to review the imperfect of *finir*."

Review the FLICS category numbers to be sure you know them. Decide on who will be the teacher, who will be the pupil, and who will be the observer. The observer will step in if he

thinks the other two are speaking different categories from those
called for. *Each column is a separate exercise. When you
finish one column, you have finished that round. Change roles
and proceed to the next column.* When most of the class has
finished, go over this exercise as a total class, hearing some of
the possibilities from the various trios.

role play I	role play II	role play III	role play IV	role play V	role play VI
5	1	7b	4a	5	5
6	5	9	8	4b	4a
9	4d	2b	2a	9	9
2b	8	4b	4c	3	2b
6	9	8	8	4b	7b
2a	3	3	3	8	
4a	3	3	4d	3	
8	3		8		
2a			3		

Skill Session V—Using Audiotapes, Videotapes, or Films

If you are teaching, then it is most worthwhile to tape
yourself, and listen, using the FLICS numbers to record and
analyze the classroom talk. These tapes need not be long; they
might be about twenty minutes worth of teaching. If you bring
them to class and the total class listens, then the tape should be
stopped frequently to check whether there is agreement on the
numbers being tallied. If enough tape recorders are available,
then the class can divide into small groups to listen and tally,
and again the tapes should be stopped for discussion quite
frequently. Just write the FLICS numbers as they occur.

If you are not teaching and personal tapes are not available, you can practice tallying classroom behavior using video-
tapes, films, or audiotapes. Audiotapes are easy to obtain;
merely ask a number of teachers if they will contribute a tape,
which can be kept completely anonymous.

When class members bring in their own tapes, these should *not* be graded—they are brought as contributions to the class. If class members are willing, their tapes can be discussed in terms of suggested change but the discussion should avoid making people defensive.

When tallying behavior, just write the numbers as they occur. The more usual method is to tally a number every three seconds, except when the behavior changes, in which case the new number is written immediately whether or not the three-second period is up. Then a matrix is constructed showing all the tallies.[4] However, this is rather a complex process and not necessary for our purposes.

Skill Session IV—Using the FLICS To Tally Directly in Classrooms

If you are a teacher, it will be easy for you to arrange to visit fellow-teachers to observe their classroom talk. Undergraduates will sometimes have to have arrangements made for them so that they can go into schools for this purpose. Teachers who are being observed can be told the exact purpose of the assignments, or if you think this is too threatening, you can say that your assignment is to observe classroom climate. As you listen and observe, write the FLICS numbers as they occur, so that you become continuously more aware of classroom talk.

Skill Session VII—Microteaching

Microteaching consists of teaching something to a small group of people for a short period of time, then analyzing the teaching and reteaching the same content to a different small group if not satisfied with the results. That is, the teacher teaches one concept or one small bit of a lesson to from one to five

[4] Ned Flanders, *Analyzing Teaching Behavior* (Reading, Mass.: Addison-Wesley Publishing Company, Inc., 1970).

persons and then analyzes what happened, using videotape, audiotape, or an observer's feedback. If after the analysis session the teacher has not achieved what he wanted, he tries again with from one to five different pupils and then analyzes that; if necessary he tries again, and so on. The important part of the analysis session, I believe, is to use some system for analyzing the teaching—not merely to talk about relatively unimportant matters like using a magnet board rather than a flannel board or writing on the chalkboard in more regular lines.

If you can microteach using videotape, fine. If not, tape recorders are usually available, and these are helpful. If you have neither, you can have your teaching behavior tallied by an observer.

Skill Session VIIA—Microteaching in the College Classroom

Divide into groups of four and plan a lesson of five minutes duration. Then decide upon one person to be the teacher and join with another group who will serve as pupils. Group 1, for example, will be the first group to teach their lessons. One member of group 1 will act as teacher and the other three members will be observers who tally behavior. The four members of group 2 will be the pupils. The teacher from group 1 will teach for five minutes and then get feedback—from the pupils as well as the observers. Feedback can last for about ten or fifteen minutes and will be longer if audio- or videotape is used, because the playback takes time. If the teacher wants to try again, then group 4 will serve as pupils for group 1. This exercise can be used many times in order for everyone to have a turn.

Always remember that the teacher should use the evidence presented to evaluate himself on the basis of his goals. Observers should strive for the presentation of objective evidence for the teacher to examine. The feelings of the pupils are a part of the evidence—as are the feelings of the teacher. The audio- or videotape, of course, will help in deciding what categories were used, because they can be used to retrieve talk that is in question.

Skill Session VIIB—Microteaching with Children

For this skill session you must have access to children; either you go to a school, or, if it can be arranged, a group of children can be brought to the college. You need enough children so that when you reteach you teach to a different group. Again, plan some lessons in groups and take turns being the teacher. The other members of the planning group, who do not serve as teacher, participate as observers who tally the teacher's and pupils' behavior using the FLICS. Again use audio- or videotape if you have this, in conjunction with the FLICS. If not, use live observation and feedback alone.

This completes the skill session section using the FLICS. We will look next at some other systems for formulating classroom questions.

Questions Based on the Work of Hilda Taba

Hilda Taba has a hierarchy of teaching strategies for developing thinking, from simple operations to complex.[5] The Taba system contains eliciting questions, which lead to covert mental operations, which lead, in turn, to overt activity. The categories are presented in Table 2.

Using the Taba Categories

Ordinarily one would use the Taba question categories over an extended unit or series of lessons, building slowly from one level to another. The following example of a classroom situation in which all the categories are used is presented in a single lesson so that you may more easily observe the use of the varying

[5] "Implementing Thinking as an Objective in Social Studies," 37th Yearbook, National Council for the Social Studies, 1967, pp. 25–49.

TABLE 2

Hilda Taba's Three Categories of Thought Processes or Cognitive Tasks

I—concept formation

overt activity	covert mental operation	eliciting questions
A. Enumeration and listing	A. Differentiation	A. What did you see? hear? note?
B. Grouping	B. Identifying common properties, abstracting	B. What belongs together? on what criterion?
C. Labeling, categorizing, subsuming	C. Determining the hierarchical order of items	C. How would you call these groups? What belongs under what?

II—interpretation of data

overt activity	covert mental operation	eliciting questions
A. Identifying points	A. Differentiation	A. What did you note? find?
B. Explaining items of identified information	B. Relating points to each other; determining cause and effect relations	B. Why did so-and-so happen?
C. Making inferences, generalizations	C. Going beyond what is given; finding implications, extrapolating	C. What does this mean? What picture does it create in your mind? What would you conclude?

III—application of principles

overt activity	covert mental operation	eliciting questions
A. Predicting consequences; explaining unfamiliar phenomena; hypothesizing	A. Analyzing the nature of the problem or situation; retrieving relevant knowledge	A. What would happen if? What idea might account for?
B. Explaining, supporting the predictions and hypotheses	B. Determining the causal links leading to prediction or hypotheses	B. Why do you think this would happen?
C. Verifying the prediction	C. Using logical methods or factual knowledge to determine necessary and sufficient conditions	C. What would it take for so-and-so to be true or probably true? or not true?

levels of questions. Eliciting questions that lead to Taba's overt activities are named, numbered, and italicized.

Names and Places—A Seventh Grade Lesson

Miss Casey began the activity with her seventh grade class by saying, "Let's pretend that each of us is going to found a new town or city in a brand new place, where no settlement has ever been before. Take a few minutes to think about the name you would choose, and when you have it, write it down." After a few minutes, Miss Casey asked, "Did everyone have a chance to think of something? All right, take a moment to tell your neighbor what you have chosen." (This is done to give everyone a chance to be heard, since everyone may not have a chance to share with the total class.)

IA—Listing: "Now, let's hear some of the choices."
As the students called out their choices, three other students listed them on the board, so that the teacher could give her full attention to the class.

The youngsters choices for names were: Happyville, Richville, Mountain City, Pattysville, Peace City, Robintown, Goldsville, NoWorkland, Gardentown, Tom's Place, Spring Valley, Funtown, Goodland, Ocean View, Nice Place, Pretty City, Candyland, Theresaville, My Town, Utopia, New America, Space City, and Grassy Place.

IB—Grouping: "Do any of these names we have chosen go together in any way?" asked Miss Casey. *"Do some seem to belong together, and why do you think so?"*

"Well, all the ones that end in 'ville' go together because they all end the same way."

"All right, let's put a check next to those that have 'ville' as their suffix."

"Some of them sound like they'd be nice places to be, so I think they belong together, like Grassy Place, Nice Place, Goldsville, Pretty City, Peace City, and Utopia."

"Then let's put a circle by those that you're saying sound as if they'd be pleasant places to live. Any others?"

"Well, I think that NoWorkland and Candyland and Goodland go together, and so do the ones that end in 'city' like Peace City and Pretty City."

"And so do the ones that end in 'town' like Robintown, My Town, Gardentown, and Funtown," added another pupil.

"Okay, let's put checks next to all the ones with similar suffixes and add a '1' beside those that end in 'ville,' a '2' beside those that end in 'land,' and so on."

"Pattysville and Tom's Place and Theresaville go together because they all have people's names in them."

"We'll put triangles next to those that seem to belong to or be named after people."

"Some have scenery in them, like Mountain City or Grassy

Place or Spring Valley, or Ocean View, so I think they go together."

"We'll put a star next to those names, then, that seem to describe some scenery we'd see if we went to those places."

"I think Richville and Goldsville go together because they're both about money."

"Okay, how about an X next to those. Any others? Well, I think we have enough to move on to our next question."

IC—Labeling: "What can we call these different groups? What names could we give, for example, to all the things we have listed next to the X's or the checks or circles?"

"The ones with the checks could all be called 'same ending names.' "

"Or we could just say, 'ville names' or 'town names,' or like that."

"They could be called 'suffix names.' "

"Fine, those are all possibilities. How about the ones with circles? Those are Pretty City, Peace City, Utopia, Nice Place, Funtown, and so on."

"We could call those 'good names.' "

"Or 'good feeling names.' "

"Those are names that make you want to go there."

"Okay, how about the ones with stars, like Mountain City and Grassy Place?"

"Those tell about what's in those places."

"Yeah, they tell about the scenery, so they could be 'scenery names.' "

This discussion continued until many possible categories had been discussed. According to Taba, all possibilities should be accepted. Thus names can be classified under several different headings, and it is important that children understand that names are classified differently by different people.

"You know," Miss Casey said to the class after they had finished the grouping of names, "other people—experts—have done what we have just done; that is, they have thought about place names, and they have classified them in much the way that we have. The names that we have put stars next to, our 'scenery names,' are called *descriptive* names; and names that have people's names are called *possessive* names, unless they are in honor of these people, and then they are called *commemorative* names. Our 'New America' is a commemorative name, and these kinds of names account for the largest number of place names. These are places named after people, other places, or events. If Theresaville means it belongs to Theresa, then it's a possessive name, but if it's named in honor of Theresa, then it's a commemorative name. The ones we have called 'good names' are called *euphemistic* names, and these names are usually given to places where people hope they will find good things. We'll come back to these words later, but for now, I think it's just interesting to know that experts have grouped place names very much as we have."

Next Miss Casey displayed a map of the United States showing the distribution of "Buffalo" as a place name.[6] "The circles on this map, and there are over a hundred of them, all have the same name. Some are the names of cities, some of towns or counties, and some are names of physical features like streams. See if you can make a guess about what this name is?" (The name is virtually impossible to guess, since the largest clustering of names is east of the Mississippi.)

"They could all have 'town' or 'city' in them."

"That's a good possibility, and an excellent hunch, but they don't have anything like that—they have just one name."

"Is it somebody's name, like Lincoln?"

"That's another good guess, but that isn't what these circles are named."

"They all have 'New' in them, I bet."

"Well, that's a good hunch too, and like all the others is based on sound thinking. Well, it would be almost impossible to guess this, so I'm going to tell you. It's 'Buffalo!' "

After many, "whats!" "wows!" and other exclamations, the class talked about the distribution of the name "Buffalo" on the map.

[6] "What's Behind a Place Name?" *Cartocraft Teaching Aids,* Vol. III, No. 2, Series 1962–1963, based on the work of George R. Stewart.

IIA—Identifying Points: "What do you notice about where these names are found?" asked Miss Casey.

"Well, all over the place."

"Look how many are in the east!"

IIB—Explaining Items of Identified Information: "Why is this so? Why are so many places named Buffalo?" Miss Casey inquired of the class.

"Well, because people don't have too many good ideas, so they use the same name over and over."

"It must be because there were buffalo in these places. But I thought the buffalo lived only in the West."

"Yeah, me too," came from most of the class.

"Under this map which I showed you, it says that buffalo were seen in North Carolina and Virginia, and evidently in these other places, and people named streams and so on after them. It is sort of a surprise, because we do think of the buffalo as having lived on the Western plains only," Miss Casey said. "Anyway, you're saying that people named the places 'Buffalo' because they saw buffalo there, and that probably makes them fall in which category that we talked about before? Yes, descriptive names—because there were buffalo *seen* in those places. It's no longer descriptive of most of these places, but it once was. Can you think of other names that may have once been descriptive but no longer have whatever is described?"

"Yes—my street. It's called Oak Street, but there aren't any trees on the whole street anymore. My mother told me why it was named Oak Street—because there used to be a lot of oak trees around."

IIC—Making Generalizations: "What are some of the things we can conclude now after our discussion about places and names? Talk for a while in your small groups of three before we talk about this as a whole class."

After allowing several minutes for pupils to share ideas in the smaller groups, Miss Casey said, "Okay, now that we've had some time to talk together, let's see what we have to say about place names. What are some of your conclusions?"

"Well, a lot of places have names because of what people

saw when they came there. Like buffalo—people saw those animals, so they named the places that."

"Well, our group concluded about buffalo that there used to be many of them around before people killed them off— which was too bad."

IIC—Making Inferences: "What can you say, then, about names which places have now that when we think about them don't seem to mean much?" asked Miss Casey.

"Well, names tell something about a place, but maybe the name might tell about it a long time ago—like it means something back in history."

"So names have some sort of story to tell about places," said Miss Casey.

"Well, our group talked about the names we chose ourselves, and most of those were about what we wished would be there. Like something good, or some good feeling. Something like that name you said before."

"You're saying that many of our personal choices for place names were euphemistic—they were about the future and the good things we hoped would be there. That's interesting, too, because there aren't many of these kinds of place names, really. Most place names are about the present or the past— and most of ours were about the future. Later maybe it would be interesting to discuss that. Any other conclusions you came to about naming?"

"Our group noticed that different people chose names for different reasons."

"But a lot of the names are alike—we saw how many 'Buffalos' there are, and while lots of names were different in our class, we picked them for the same reasons—like our own name, or what we want."

"So," said Miss Casey, "people pick names for a number of different reasons, and so there are many, many different place names. But people also pick names for similar reasons, so there are also many places with the same name. And people have different things in mind when they choose a name."

IIC—Making Inferences: "Did any of you think about why people give names to places at all?"

"Well, places have to have names. Otherwise, how would you know where anything is?"

"Yeah, if nothing had names, then nobody would know where they live, and everybody would be getting lost and everything like that."

"They give names so you can tell one place from another, that's why."

"So people name places to identify these places and to differentiate one place from another," said Miss Casey. "Let me ask you something else."

IIC—Making Generalizations: "Do places have names that absolutely belong to them, and have always been used?"

"No—no place has a name till people give it a name. If nobody is in a place, it doesn't have a name."

"Yeah, like we were talking about before, with the places on the moon. They don't have names yet for a lot of the places there, because we didn't give them names."

"Nothing has a name unless people give it—furniture or anything else."

"Okay, then nothing has names until names are given by people," Miss Casey said. "We wouldn't have names, unless our parents had given us names. And schools, streets, oceans, camps, grocery stores—everything that has a name—was named by a person or a group of people. And every name has a story behind it. For example, you were given a name for a certain reason, and one thing I'd like you to do for homework tonight is to write a short paper on your name. Why were you given your particular name, and so on. You might have to interview someone in your family to get this information, or you might already know, but let's hold discussion on that until tomorrow."

"So," continued Miss Casey, "we've concluded a number of different things. That different people choose names for different reasons, and sometimes for the same reasons. If places didn't have names, it would be hard to find our way around and to tell one place from another. And we found that places don't have names on their own—they are given names by people."

"Well, I thought of something else, Miss Casey. People can

change the names of places too. Like New York used to be New Amsterdam."

"Yeah, and before that it was Manhattan, and maybe it was something else before that that we don't even know."

IIC—Making Inferences: "Do you think that some day New York might have a different name?" asked Miss Casey.

"Maybe if a different kind of people live here some day they might pick a different name."

"Some day it might have a name like Space Stop 5, or something like that."

"All right," said Miss Casey. "Now let's move on to something else."

IIIA—Predicting Consequences: "Suppose that suddenly the government decreed that overnight all place names had to commemorate important national events or honor national heroes or presidents. What would happen?"

"Well, I wouldn't do it. It wouldn't be fair."

"I agree with you that it wouldn't be very logical, but just for the sake of thinking about it, let's pretend that it was so, and we were willing to cooperate. What would happen?" Miss Casey asked again.

"People would have to decide on what names to pick, and they'd argue about that."

IIIB—Explaining the Prediction: "Why would they argue?" asked the teacher.

"Because one person might think that it should be named after one hero and some people would think it should be named after another, and some people would think it should be named after a battle and other people would think it should be named after something good, like what we were studying about polio vaccine discovery."

"So there might be many arguments about names, and also about *how* to name. Who *should* do it?" inquired Miss Casey.

"Well, that's what I was wondering about. How could we

decide who would pick the names, and should there be votes about it, and all that?"

"Well, another thing is that after the names were changed everybody would be very mixed up for a long time, and you wouldn't know where anything was."

IIIB—Explaining the Prediction: "Why is that?" asked Miss Casey.

"Well, suppose you had to remember new names for everything—it would be too hard. If they were talking about this place and that place and you never heard of them, you wouldn't know where they were talking about."

"Yeah, or if you had to go to someplace, how would you get there? You'd have to have all new maps."

"But you'd have to have all the old names, too, or you still couldn't get there, because people wouldn't know all of the new names for awhile."

IIIA—Predicting Consequences: "What would happen if places didn't have any names at all?" asked Miss Casey.

"You could never find anything, because nobody could tell you where anything was."

"They could describe how to get there—like say it's near the red house on the corner."

"That wouldn't do any good—it would be too hard, unless the place were right near."

"You could number places instead of naming them."

"Well, that might help, but there's not enough numbers, and how could you remember them anyway?"

"Besides, then a number would be a name—so the places would still have names."

"You're saying, then," said Miss Casey, "that it would be pretty hard to find our way around if places didn't have names; that while we might try describing how to get somewhere without using names, it would be very difficult, especially if the place were far away; and that naming places in some other way, with numbers, for example, would still be using names."

IIIC—Verifying the Prediction: "Can anybody try telling us how to get from your house to school without using any names at

all—no street names of any kind? Try this in your small groups
of three and see how it goes."

The youngsters did this in small groups and found that the
farther from school one lived, the more difficult the assignment
was. They decided that one consequence of places without names
would be that people would tend to stay in their own neighborhoods, because otherwise they might get lost. Another possibility
might be that people would have to develop better memories
to remember exactly where they traveled, so they could find
their way back.

*IIIC—Verifying the Prediction: "Is there any other kind of ex-
periment we could do here in school to verify the fact that a
lack of names would make things difficult?* You can think about
any names—place names, people names, or names of things. In
your small groups see what ideas you come up with."

What the class finally decided upon to test the consequences
of not using names was to spend the rest of that day without
speaking or writing any person's name or the name or number
of any room or place in or out of the school. They also decided
to write a letter to the mayor of their city and try to tell him
how to get to their school without using any place names. Need-
less to say, their prediction about the importance of names was
verified.

Skill Session IX—Identifying Categories
for Taba Questions in a Second Grade Lesson

Here is another example of a classroom activity built
around the Taba questions, this time in a second grade class.
As you read through, determine the proper category for the
italicized teacher questions.

Schools and Classrooms

"Let's spend a little time this morning," said Miss DeVita
to her second grade class, "looking around the room and noticing
what we have in here. *What do we see here in our room?"*

As the children called out their responses, the teacher wrote them on a pad initially, rather than on the board, because she could jot down what they said more quickly this way. The youngsters had a long list of items: desks, books, blocks, puzzles, windows, chalk, and so on.

"Are there other kinds of things in here—live things?" asked Miss DeVita.

"Oh yes—there's fish, and the turtle."

"And there's us."

"That's right—there's boys and girls."

"And the teacher, too, don't forget!"

"All right, then, we have a long list of things which are in our room. *Now let's see if some of these things we've been listing go together in any way. Do some things belong with other things?"* was Miss DeVita's next question.

"Well—books and paper go together because they're both paper."

"Chalk and pencils and pens and crayons go together because they're for writing."

"Tables and chairs go together."

"And so do desks, because that's all furniture."

"Puzzles and tinker toys and lotto and all those things go together because they're all games."

The children had many more combinations, and when they had run out of ideas the teacher moved on to another activity. Later she wrote their groupings on the board and reviewed them with the class.

"Now that we've read over these words on the board, some of them new ones, *let's think about what these different groups could be called.* For example, we already said a name for desks and chairs and tables . . . yes—furniture. *Now can you think of names for other groups?"* asked Miss DeVita.

Some of the labels decided upon were: people, things to work with, things that are fun, parts of the room, things to write *with,* and things to write *on.*

When this part of the activity was finished the teacher transferred the items and the labels (retaining whatever overlapping occurred) to charts for further reading practice and to refer to when needed.

For the next few days Miss DeVita read and told stories to the children about schools in other lands and schools of long ago. They also talked of the different kinds of schools—schools for older children, like high schools, even more advanced schools like colleges, and they talked of the many differences in schools— differences caused by age of pupils, by country, and by time in history.

Some of the questions Miss DeVita asked during these activities were, *"What kinds of schools are there?" "Why do younger children do different things in school than older children do?" "What can you tell from that story about the kinds of schools they had in those days?" "Why do you think that in those days most people didn't go to school?" "Why do you think you have to go to school longer to be a teacher than a clerk in a department store?" "What do you think we have here in our classroom that wasn't in a school room in the early days of this country?" "What might we have here that wouldn't be found in countries where most of the people are poor?" "What is there in this classroom that we think is important but that people in earlier days wouldn't have thought was important?"*

Later, Miss DeVita asked the children, *"What would happen if we decided to change our room in any way we please in order to make it as interesting and useful as possible?" "How might our room be different?"*

"Well, we could have a playground right here inside the room," suggested one youngster.

"And why would that be useful or interesting?" asked the teacher.

"Because it would be more fun."

"Everybody likes to go to the playground, and we'd have it right here."

"But it would be too noisy—you couldn't hear."

"Well, you could use the things quietly."

The discussion continued along these lines for quite a while, and then Miss DeVita asked the class, *"How could we find out if these suggestions would really make the room more interesting and useful?"*

"Well, some things we couldn't do, like we couldn't have a playground inside."

"We could too—the kindergarten has a slide in the room, and we could have some other things besides."

"We could have more books, and we could get more easels like we said."

"We could invite more people to talk to us, like Joe said, and we could have more trips."

"We could decorate the room better, and we could have that bulletin board for everybody to put anything on that they wanted."

"We could change seats every week or every month or something."

"We could trade puzzles and other stuff with other classes so we'd have new things in here all the time."

There were a number of other suggestions for discovering whether or not the room would be more interesting with certain changes, and the class determined to make the changes within the next few days to test them out—all the ones that were possible, that is.

Skill Session X—Categorizing Taba Questions in a Lesson about Television

Here is one more example of questions built around the Taba categories. This time only the teacher questions will be presented. Determine the Taba category for each question.

1. What are your favorite television programs?
2. What programs do you watch whenever you have the chance, and which do you just watch some of the time?
3. Do any of these programs that we have listed here go together in any way?
4. Why do you say those three belong together?

5. Can we give names to these groupings we've made?
6. Here is a list of the fifteen most popular television programs according to a recent poll. What do you notice about these programs?
7. Why do you think these are the most popular rather than some other programs?
8. Why do you think some of our choices were the same as theirs and some were different?
9. What can you infer from this information—what does it mean?
10. Suppose we were to take a poll to find out what television programs are popular and we asked different groups of people—college students, kindergarten children, old people, and so on. What do you think their choices would be like?
11. Why do you say that their choices would differ?
12. How can we verify these things we've predicted about the choices of different people?
13. Pretend that you gained control of all television stations but you didn't approve of television. You didn't want people to watch television, but you weren't allowed to just close the stations. What kinds of programs would you schedule to make sure that as few people as possible watched? What would you show?
14. Why would you show those particular programs?
15. Is there any way of finding out whether these kinds of programs would really prove to be so unpopular that no one would watch?

Skill Session XI—Building Your Own Questions Based on Taba's Categories

Get into small groups, according to grades or subject matter which you teach or plan to teach, and build a series of questions based on the Taba classification system. Use any content you think is appropriate.

Building a Unit on What People Need To Know

The Taba category system is useful when building units of work, because her questions are of a hierarchical nature, from simple to complex, and can be referred to for help in developing thinking skills throughout the development of the unit of work.

Taba has said that teachers should think of the *main ideas* they wish to communicate to children when teaching,[7] saying to themselves, *"What is it I want the pupils to remember when they have forgotten everything else?"* If you do this every time you teach you will be more apt to prepare teaching plans that deal with important topics and you will move away from lessons that involve memorization of unimportant facts. For example, instead of expecting pupils to memorize the capitals of the fifty states, which most youngsters will then forget, and which involves unnecessary information to begin with, you would be more apt to plan a lesson around *how* to find the names of capitals, the reasons for having capitals in states and countries, the services that are found there, the advantages and disadvantages of centralization of services, and so on.

A small sample of a possible opening lesson for the unit "What People Need To Know" follows. The opening lesson will be preceded by a list of main ideas for the unit and followed by a list of possible activities that could be included in this unit. Formulating main ideas will encourage you to take the time to think about what ideas and generalizations are to be stressed during the development of the unit—what you want the pupils to remember when they've forgotten everything else.

Main Ideas for What People Need To Know

1. All people need to know how to do many things.
2. Certain kinds of knowledge and skills are needed by all people, no matter where they live or what they do.

[7] Hilda Taba. Informal meeting, Chicago, 1967.

3. In some places in the world it is necessary to know things that are not necessary to know in other places.
4. In every society, certain knowledge and skills are needed only by certain people.
5. What people need to know can be learned in many different ways.
6. People learn what they need to know in many places, from many people: at home, in special places like schools, from friends and playmates, from radio, television, movies, and so forth.

The opening lesson (which is just one possibility out of many) presents the objectives in *behavioral* form—that is, the objectives say what it is the *pupils* will do or what product they will produce as a result of the planned procedures. The procedures lead to the accomplishment of the objectives and include the teacher's planned talk, especially questions.

First Teaching Plan for What People Need To Know

specific objectives	*procedures*
1. The children will list the things *they* need to know in order to stay alive, such as: how to talk to other people, how to get food, how to keep warm in cold weather, and so forth. (Achievement of objective to be determined by observation of verbal behavior and examination of product [the lists].)	1a. Teacher: Today we're going to begin our new social studies unit—"What People Need To Know"—and I thought we might start by talking about what *we* actually need to know in order to stay alive. I'm going to ask you to get together in groups of four to talk about this. Make a list on paper, if you can, or keep the ideas in your heads if you need to. We'll spend about five minutes on this.

specific objectives   *procedures*

b. The teacher divides the children into groups, decided upon in advance, and moves about from group to group during the discussion.

c. Teacher: All right, let's all turn so that we can face the board, and we'll hear some of the ideas. I'll list them, and we'll start by hearing one idea from each group.

d. Ideas are listed on the board— all ideas are accepted.

2. The children will rank the ideas listed as being necessary for staying alive, according to their importance. (Achievement of objective to be determined by examination of product.)

2a. Teacher: This seems to be quite a good list. Let's see if we can talk about whether or not some of these are more important than others and put numbers beside the most important, the next most important, and so on. Perhaps we'll need to add to the list as we talk about these things, or perhaps we'll take some out.

b. Who will pick the one he thinks is most important and tell us why—anyone?

Some Possible Activities for What People Need To Know

If you stop to think about what you remember from your elementary or secondary school days, the likelihood is that what pops into your mind (discounting incidents in which you were shamed, embarrassed, or treated unfairly) will be some kind of activity—like being in a play, going on a trip, constructing something in the classroom. Each of us is proof that what had impact on us in terms of school learning were things that really engaged us, that actively involved us. The following list is compiled to indicate the kinds of activities which may be included in this unit to engage pupils actively in their studies.

1. Have committees which demonstrate that different things are learned differently: one committee might teach a manual skill, one a thinking skill, one a social skill about getting along in committee work (by role-playing), and so forth.

2. Compare what people need to know in three current societies: a primitive desert people, people in your city, and people in a rural farm area in the United States. This comparison could concentrate just on what children need to know.

3. Make up a play with three episodes: a school scene showing the teaching of children in prehistoric times, in the present time, and sometime in the future when many things (cooking, much of teaching, many jobs) might be automated.

4. Compare and contrast the knowledge and skills needed by people in different jobs.

5. Investigate the means by which people are trained for different jobs.

6. Make a book collection of materials that tell about different jobs.

7. Speculate on what would happen if certain occupations disappeared from your city.

8. Compare the necessity of various kinds of jobs for the good of everyone.

9. Make a book of occupations: pictures, needed skills, training required, and so forth.

10. Compare what everyone in your city needs to know with what certain people such as teachers, policemen, grocery store owners, and so forth, need to know.

11. Make a list of what everyone in the world needs to know.
12. Role-play helpful and nonhelpful means of teaching various kinds of things.
13. Plan a program (programmed learning) which would teach another class, in small linear steps, what things are essential for people to know in order to survive.
14. Suppose you were the only person left in the world—what would you need to know? What would you no longer need (such as social skills)?
15. Suppose you suddenly moved to a very primitive society—such as the one discussed earlier under item 2. What could you teach people there that would improve their lives?
16. Compare the importance of knowing how to cooperate with knowing how to compete in a variety of situations.
17. Pretend that you have children of your own—of your age—what would you like them to know?
18. Suggest things that could be learned at school but aren't at this time. Do the same for families and groups of friends.
19. Invent new kinds of organizations for teaching certain kinds of things to children.
20. Compare a classroom (city, family) in which everyone knows how to get along with and help others with one where there is much arguing and where people pick on each other.

The stress in this unit was on main ideas, behavioral objectives, and procedures, which include teacher talk (particularly questions) and activities. There are, of course, the additional steps of how to determine if the objectives have been reached and the steps which I call "what happened" and "where do we go from here," which are dealt with after the teaching has been completed. Briefly, the planning steps may be summarized as follows:

1. What will we study?
2. Why will we study this?
3. What are the main ideas to be communicated? (What should be remembered when all else is forgotten?)
4. What specific pupil behavioral objectives will be achieved?
5. What means will be used to determine *if* these objectives have been achieved?
6. What procedures will be used to arrive at the objectives?
7. What happened?
8. Where do we go from here?

Skill Session XII—Developing Portions of Units on Your Own

Here are some possible topics for developing units, which, like "What People Need To Know," are broad enough so they can be used with a variety of age levels.

1. What it means to be human
2. Why people move about the earth
3. The groups that people belong to
4. The differences between children and adults

Using one of these topics, or selecting one of your own, work together in small groups to develop the main ideas and the first two lessons, giving special attention to questions. In addition, list all the *activities* you can think of which could be included in the unit. If you have time to work on this over an extended time, continue to develop the unit past the introductory lessons. If at all possible, the units should be taught to children as they are developed. You can teach the lessons to small groups of children; a total class is not necessary.

This completes the chapter on questioning—with one final reminder. *Pupils* should be encouraged to ask questions and to develop, or redevelop, their abilities to ask productive and provocative questions. So, in addition to working on developing your own questioning ability, put some time and energy into helping youngsters ask: Who? What? Where? When?—and more important, How? and Why?

Selected References

Dwight Allen and Kevin Ryan. *Microteaching*, Reading, Mass.: Addison-Wesley Publishing Company, Inc., 1969.

Edmund Amidon and Elizabeth Hunter. *Improving Teaching: The Analysis of Classroom Verbal Interaction*, New York: Holt, Rinehart and Winston, Inc., 1966.

Ned Flanders. *Analyzing Teaching Behavior*, Reading, Mass.: Addison-Wesley Publishing Company, Inc., 1970.

Robert Mager. *Preparing Instructional Objectives*, Palo Alto: Fearon Publishers, 1962.

Norris Sanders. *Classroom Questions: What Kinds?*, New York: Harper & Row, Publishers, 1966.

Hilda Taba and others. *Social Studies Units, Grades 1–6*, Hayward, Calif.: Rapid Printers and Lithographers, Inc., 1965.

making the scene:
arranging for effective
classroom communication

written with the cooperation of Linda Lantieri*

Children's classroom behavior is not just the result of the particular mix of pupils who happen to be placed together for the year; nor is it simply the result of the individual backgrounds pupils bring with them to school. Of course, these factors have an effect, but much pupil behavior is the direct result of teacher

* Linda Lantieri, at the time of this writing has had a year and a half of teaching experience, all in the fifth grade at P.S. 171 in New York City. She studied with me as an undergraduate and graduate student and is, I believe, an outstanding teacher—creative, courageous, and dedicated.

behavior. For example, the teacher who does not share power with pupils, constantly reprimands them, uses ridicule and sarcasm, pits classmates against each other, and creates a competitive rather than a collaborative climate is encouraging certain kinds of behavior in youngsters. This teacher will probably have more than the usual amount of classroom tattling (anyone who can point out the misbehavior of others may be momentarily in the good graces of the "boss"), pupils will laugh at others who get the answers wrong (even though anyone's turn for ridicule may be next, important momentary satisfaction can be obtained from feeling superior to others), and the classroom will be one in which pupils are afraid to ask for help or indicate that they don't understand (protecting oneself from criticism is far more important than comprehending assigned work).

On the other hand, the teacher who creates a warm and supportive climate by making a place for everyone and by honestly sharing power with youngsters encourages pupils to receive satisfaction from each others' achievements, and, in fact, to help each other in realizing these achievements. (In many classrooms, sharing ideas or answers is defined as cheating!) Children can afford to recognize their classmates' success because everyone will have many successes; they don't need to laugh at each others' mistakes because they know that mistakes are acceptable—that it's all right to make evident what they don't know. Communication will be more open and effective and will result in a higher level of cognitive and affective learning.

This chapter describes some of the specific ways in which the behavior of one teacher, Linda Lantieri, helped her fifth graders become more open in their communication. Miss Lantieri's ideas were generally supported by her school administration, but the most important factor in the evolution of the many-faceted curriculum she developed with her class of Black and Puerto Rican youngsters was her own determination to help her pupils learn to help themselves and each other. There were twenty-four children in this essentially self-contained classroom. Toward the end of the year a paraprofessional joined them, and during the year several student teachers were placed in the class.

There were also four specialists who worked with the class, each once a week for one period.

The unit of study described in these pages specifically deals with the improvement of classroom communication. The purpose of the unit was to upgrade discussion in general and to introduce "group meetings," which were used throughout the year to encounter and explore problems and feelings. While Miss Lantieri taught this unit at the beginning of the year, it could be introduced at any time, with individual lessons covered daily, weekly, or in any way which seems feasible.

Improving Classroom Communication: A Unit

Lesson 1—Forming Groups

Very soon after school started in the fall, Miss Lantieri began a unit with her fifth grade class designed to make classroom discussions more effective and satisfying. For this first lesson, the entire class was seated in a circle, as they would be for most encounters during the year. Tables and desks were pushed back against the walls, and the children gathered in a circle, often sitting on the floor, sometimes sitting on chairs; and usually each child chose as neighbors in the circle whomever he wished.

"This year we're going to be having discussions about many things," began Miss Lantieri, "both as a total class and in small groups, and since we're going to spend so much time talking to each other, or communicating with each other, it seems logical to learn how to have the best possible discussions. So we're going to spend quite a bit of time during the next few weeks learning about ways we can communicate more effectively in this classroom. I said before that some of the time we'd be working in small groups. Why are small groups useful sometimes?"

"Well, you get more chance to talk that way."

"It's more fun."

"You can do different things—like every group can talk about something different."

"You learn more that way."

A number of other suggestions were made, and then Miss Lantieri said, "These are *all* possible reasons for working in small groups. Now—what are some ways we might divide into these groups? How can we actually split up?"

"Well, *you* could decide and call out the names."

"The people who sit near each other could be a group."

"We could decide between ourselves who to be with."

After several other suggestions were offered, Miss Lantieri noted that some of the time she might form the groups and at other times the class might get into groups by choosing in a number of different ways.

"Today," she continued, "we're going to try several ways of forming groups. We have twenty-four people, so if we wanted groups of six, how many groups would we have? Yes, four. First, I'm going to ask four people to stand up and move about the room to begin to choose people for a group. They'll just walk up to someone and say, 'I'd like you to be in my group,' and then together they'll go to another person and the second person will say, 'I choose you' to the third, and then the third person will pick someone he wants, and so on, until there are six people. When the group has been completed just stand together until everyone has been chosen. Let's have these four people begin."

When this had been done and the groups were formed, Miss Lantieri said, "All right, now, take a few moments to tell each other some of the ways you felt about choosing and being chosen—just standing wherever you are." While the groups talked, Miss Lantieri moved from group to group making an occasional nonjudgmental comment, such as, "You felt glad when you were chosen," or, "You thought maybe nobody would ever get to you, and you felt worried."

"Let's come back into the big circle now," said Miss Lantieri after a few minutes for small group talk, "and hear what some of the different feelings were."

Quite a few children spoke of their pleasure or concern,

and Miss Lantieri's conversation consisted almost entirely of questions or nonjudgmental comments of acceptance. When a number of youngsters had had an opportunity to speak, Miss Lantieri asked, "Can you think of another way to form small groups—without using words at all?"

"You could just go up to people and touch them."

"You could signal to them—like waving or something."

"You could just look at the people you wanted."

"Let's try a couple of those ways. First, let's try just touching people. I'll ask four different people to choose, and they'll go up to people and touch them in some way, and then these people will join hands. For example, Johnny might go up to Hector and touch him, and he'll stand and take Johnny's hand, and they'll move on to someone whom Hector will touch, and then three people will be holding hands, and so on, until there are six. When you have six, close your circle by all joining hands; that way we'll know that your group is completed. Okay, the four peoples who start things off will be. . . ."

When the circles were completed, the children were again asked to tell each other how they felt about being chosen in this way. Some groups continued to hold hands while they spoke, others did not.

When they were seated again in the large circle and shared feelings, some children who hadn't spoken before did so this time. Many seemed to like this method of forming groups, saying it was different and fun. Some of the boys, however, expressed discomfort and said they thought the door should be locked if this method were used. "What if the principal walked in? He would wonder what we were doing," and a number of similar comments led them ultimately to understand, with some help from the teacher in the form of probing questions, that they were afraid to have outsiders see them holding hands with other boys. They themselves thought it was all right, but they worried about being seen. However, since they really thought this was a good method for forming groups, it was finally decided that since they were holding hands for a good reason, it really didn't matter—but it *would* be better to have the door locked.

"Now we've tried one verbal way of getting into groups

and one nonverbal way. Let's try another nonverbal way—another way where we don't use words. The people doing the selecting will just look at the people they want, one at a time, until each group has six. Let's have these people begin the choosing. . . ." and Miss Lantieri designated four different youngsters.

In the total group discussion about this particular method, some of the comments were, "Why didn't you get up when I looked at you?"

"Well, I didn't think you were really looking at me, because you looked away kind of fast."

"I looked away because I didn't think you wanted to be in my group, because you didn't get up."

"Well, I didn't get up because you looked away!"

"Yeah, that happened to me too—I didn't know if people were going to get up."

"Sounds as if some of us want to be very sure we're wanted before we'll join," commented Miss Lantieri.

"Using eyes is much harder than the touch way."

After more discussion on this topic, Miss Lantieri concluded with, "That's all we're going to do with this for now. We've been communicating with each other with words and without words—in verbal and nonverbal ways. How did you feel about what we did today?" After some discussion which indicated that the children liked the activities, Miss Lantieri continued, "Tomorrow we're going to talk about what actually makes discussions interesting, and maybe we'll use some of these ways of getting into small groups when that's called for."

"Oh good! Let's use the nonverbal one with touch."

"Yeah, that was a good one!"

(Depending upon the size of the class and the purpose of the activity, the number and size of groups will vary. For example, a class of thirty might have ten groups of three for one purpose and six groups of five for another.)

Nonverbal group formation using touch was used extensively in Miss Lantieri's class, and she found closing the circle as a sign that the group was ready to be a useful device, since each group was eager to finish and, thus, everyone was quickly included. As time went on and there were continual discussions about feelings, many children purposely selected classmates on the second or third round who might ordinarily be chosen last, because they learned to empathize with one another and wanted to help classmates who suffered from "last" feelings.

The teacher must always be sensitive to what is happening, sometimes selecting children to initiate the choosing who might not be selected until toward the end, selecting all girls at times so that mixed groups will result more easily (since there will not be enough girls in the class for each selector to choose only other girls), and making certain that feelings about the process are brought out and discussed.

Lesson 2—What Makes a Topic Interesting

Miss Lantieri began this session by reminding the class that they thought yesterday's activity and discussion were interesting and then asking them what made some discussions interesting and some discussions not so interesting. It was determined that two factors were at work; one was the topic and the other the behavior of the people doing the talking.

"What are some of the ways that people act sometimes that make discussions uninteresting?"

"Well, some kids hog everything and they never let anybody else talk."

"When kids start arguing and yelling all the time."

"Sometimes nobody else wants to talk, and I'm the only one talking, and then it's not so interesting."

"Sometimes other people start talking while I'm still talking."

"Yeah, when people talk at the same time, that's no good."

"When people don't even pay attention to me when I say something, that's not interesting."

"All right," said Miss Lantieri, "so the behavior of people in discussion groups is very important in determining whether or not the discussion will be a good one. We're going to spend quite a bit of time on behavior later on, but for now we're going to concentrate on topics. Why was yesterday's topic interesting to us?"

"Because we liked what we were doing."

"It was about us."

"Well, we found out things that are interesting about people."

"We told how we felt, and that was interesting."

"What are some topics that would not be interesting to us?" asked Miss Lantieri.

"Football isn't interesting to me to talk about," said one of the girls.

"That's just because you don't know what's interesting!" responded a boy.

"Some of the things my sister is learning in high school— they're not interesting to me. Like algebra."

"Yeah, and who cares what they're doing in the first grade—that's no fun to talk about."

"I don't think spelling is interesting."

"And math isn't interesting."

After a number of other comments Miss Lantieri summarized, "We've said that sometimes discussions are spoiled for us by the way people act, and also that some topics just aren't interesting to some of us, although they might be to others. And whether or not a topic is interesting might depend on age, on whether we're boys or girls, and so on. Can you think of anything else that might make it hard to have a good conversation?"

There wasn't much response to this, so the teacher asked why they thought things like reading were usually taught in the morning rather than later in the day.

"Oh, because that's something you really need to pay attention to, and maybe we're more wide awake in the morning."

"Yeah, later in the day we're more tired."

"So the time of day and the amount of energy you have might have something to do with whether or not you think activities or topics are interesting."

"And sometimes, if there's something *more* interesting going on you don't want to talk about anything. Like if my favorite television program is on, I don't care what anybody's talking about—I won't listen!"

"You're saying that one thing might be so interesting that

something else, even though it's sort of interesting, would be ignored, and that's an important observation.

"For the rest of the morning let's work on one of the things we've mentioned—what makes topics interesting. We're going to divide into small groups, and each group will choose one person to be the recorder to write down what the group says. Each group will think of topics it believes would be interesting for our class to discuss and the recorder will make a list. Now, how would you like to get into groups?"

"Use touch—without words," was the unanimous response.

"Okay. I'll call on four people to choose, and when your circle is closed, find a place in the room to sit down together. When you've decided upon a recorder, raise your hands. We'll have these people pick groups."

If some groups took longer than seemed necessary to choose recorders, Miss Lantieri would just select one as she moved around, saying, "Do you have a recorder yet? Well, then, Carmela, would you be willing to be the writer today?"

"Now, before we start, what is our task again? Yes, to list topics we think would be interesting to this class. I'll walk around while you're working, so if you need me just let me know."

Five or ten minutes was given to topic listing, and then Miss Lantieri asked the first recorder to read the entire list, slowly, so that the other recorders could check off anything they also had listed. This meant that the last group had very few things to add and helped the class to see that there were many things which all of them agreed would be interesting to discuss.

Some of the choices for interesting topics were smoking, sports, our brothers and sisters, what do you like to do in your spare time, what do your parents do when you do something wrong, television programs, allowances (how much do you get and how does it work out), family living (sex education), dating, homework, getting mad, and what you like about school.

"Well, it's obvious," said Miss Lantieri, "that there are many things that all of us would want to talk about. *Why* is it that we would want to talk about the things on this list?"

"Because they're about us."

"That's why we're interested, because they're things we want to know about."

"I want to know if cigarettes really make you shorter."

"I want to know more about family living. We had it last year, and it was good, but there's more things I want to know."

Miss Lantieri had listed the topics on the board as the recorders read them, and now she used this list to ask the youngsters what other groups besides this class might or might not want to discuss the various topics. As groups were identified, she listed them alongside the topics and drew lines to the topic or topics in which each might be interested.

"Well, everybody would be interested in television, because everybody watches it, and there's programs for everybody."

"Everybody's interested in smoking, because the older people who smoke they should know if it's bad, and the same for the people who are in the middle age, and the kids need to know whether they should start."

"Older people wouldn't be interested in family living, because they already know all about it."

"And older people wouldn't be interested in 'what you like about school,' because they don't go."

After listening to many comments about what would or would not be interesting to different groups, Miss Lantieri said, "We've done well, I think, in identifying some topics that we can discuss in class, and we've also done some good thinking about what kinds of topics would be interesting to different groups. For homework tonight I'd like you to decide upon three groups of people (for example, boys, little children, teachers) and then decide upon five topics. List the topics on one side of the paper and the groups on the other, and circle the groups as I did here on the board; then draw lines from the circles to the topics *if* you think the topic would be interesting to that group. Any questions?"

Lesson 3—More on What Makes Topics Interesting

The next day Miss Lantieri put the class into small groups to share the results of their homework assignment. Again the class asked to get into groups nonverbally by touch, and this continued to be the most popular way of forming groups throughout the year. The teacher began to use the nonverbal signal of turning off the lights as a signal to begin and turning them on when the groups were ready to start. The class had some interesting discussions comparing verbal and nonverbal communications, which are not included here, simply because so many things happened in this classroom that another book would be needed to describe them all.

When the groups, made up of four children this time, were seated at tables, they passed their homework lists around within the group, and when they had read each others' work, they spent a few minutes discussing the lists.

When this had been done, Miss Lantieri showed the class two boxes she had prepared and explained, "Each of these boxes contains pieces of paper with something written on them. One box has topics—one topic for each piece of paper—and the other box has groups—one group on each paper. One person at a time will come up and pick one piece of paper from the topic box and one piece from the group box. That person will read what he has chosen to the class and then bring the papers back to his group; then you'll spent a short time discussing whether or not the particular group would find the topic interesting. For example, suppose you picked for a topic, 'learning to play London Bridge,' and for a group you selected, 'a grandmothers' club.' You would discuss whether or not that topic would be a good one for that group."

The groups Miss Lantieri had selected were a grandmothers' club, a group of fifth grade boys, a kindergarten class, the teachers at our school, a parent-teacher group, our class, and storekeepers. The topics identified were hospital care, sports, how to spend a hundred dollar school fund, how to make the school a better place, how to make a store window look good to passersby, and how to help people get along with each other.

The groups spent about two minutes discussing each pair and then then another round began, with each group sending its slips to the group on its right until each group had discussed six choices. There was no total group discussion, and the teacher circulated among the groups as they talked.

Then Miss Lantieri passed out rexographed sheets which listed all the topics and all the groups, and each pupil filled in his sheet, drawing lines from the topics to the groups he thought would be interested in them.

After she had collected the sheets, Miss Lantieri suggested, "For the rest of the day, let's notice when we as a class are talking about things that are interesting and whether or not individuals are talking about matters that are interesting to us."

Later in the day a child said that something reminded her of Puerto Rico and began telling about an event which had happened there. Another child said, "You're always talking about Puerto Rico, and that's not interesting to me."

"Do you think you talk a lot about Puerto Rico?" asked Miss Lantieri.

"Well, I'm going to move back there pretty soon, so maybe I do. But I don't know."

"Well, you do," said several children.

"It's understandable that Puerto Rico is very much on your mind," said Miss Lantieri, "but perhaps you need to think about whether or not the others will be interested if you mention it too often."

A number of times the discussion moved away from the supposed topic, and that was commented upon and led to the conclusion that leaving the topic did not necessarily mean it was uninteresting. Sometimes this meant that the new direction was even *more* interesting, or had to be dealt with before the original topic could be covered.

(The learnings from every lesson in this unit were carried over into each day's work, since class discussions and small group work were a part of every area of the curriculum.)

Lesson 4—How To Bring People into the Group

"Today as we work on improving our discussion skills, we're going to do something a little different. Six people are going to sit in a smaller circle in the center while the rest of us observe their discussion. The people in the inner circle will begin by choosing a topic, and they'll have about five minutes for the discussion. So that they don't spend a lot of time deciding, whatever is mentioned first will be the topic."

Miss Lantieri then named six people to make up the inner circle and told the rest of the class, in the outer circle, that their task would be to make a tally mark each time a person spoke. That is, they would jot down the person's name or initials and make a mark next to his name whenever he said something.

A boy in the inner circle suggested the topic be football.

"Oh, that's no good," complained one of the girls.

"Well, the teacher said whatever was mentioned first was okay," was the response.

"Which do you like better, football or baseball?"

"Football, because you can play it in all kinds of weather."

"Yeah, and it's more fun to watch, because there's more going on. Baseball isn't so interesting."

"Well, I think football is more fun because it's rougher."

"Yeah, but you can get hurt more playing football."

"If you're good at football, you could get a scholarship and go to college."

"Well, the reason I like . . ."

When Miss Lantieri called a halt after about five minutes, she asked the observers for a report on how often people had spoken, and when this had been given, she asked, "What do you particularly notice about these results?"

"Well, the boys did most of the talking."

"And why did that happen?"

"The girls weren't interested in football, and they don't have anything to say on the topic."

"They don't even know anything about it, so how could they talk?"

Miss Lantieri then asked the inner circle for any comments or feelings they had, and this continued to be the general pattern when the inner circle was used—first the outer circle would give feedback and then the inner circle would react.

When the inner circle had had time to voice opinions and feelings, Miss Lantieri said, "Now let's have these same people talk again, but this time let's have them try to pick a topic that would be interesting to all the members. Anyone can suggest, but remember to try to choose something interesting and try not to spend a lot of time deciding. Maybe something else from our list would be good."

"What about how your parents punish you."

"Yeah, that's a good one," came several responses, and that became the topic.

As the outer circle tallied again, the inner circle members said things like, "My father doesn't touch me, but my mother hits me. My father just sends me to my room."

"My mother asks for my side, and then she whips me if she thinks it's my fault."

Miss Lantieri, who was sitting in the inner circle, as she usually did, asked, "Do you think it's helpful to get hit?"

"Well, I keep getting hit for the same things, and I keep doing them. I get a bad report and I get hit, but I keep on getting bad reports."

"I took my bike out when I wasn't supposed to and I got beat up for it; I never did that again."

"So sometimes hitting stops you from repeating what you've done and sometimes it doesn't," said Miss Lantieri, following her typical behavior pattern in these encounters of either asking questions or accepting responses.

"I get punished by not being let to go outside and play."

"My mother takes my allowance away."

"Yeah, that happens to me too."

"That never happens to me, I just get hit."

When Miss Lantieri indicated that time was up and the outer circle reported their tallies, the main finding was that two youngsters had hardly spoken. The teacher had purposely chosen these two very quiet youngsters as participants.

"Why do you think that some people didn't speak as often as others?" she asked.

"Maybe the topic wasn't interesting to them."

"No—everybody would be interested in that, because everybody gets punished."

"Yeah, and it's good to know what happens to other kids."

"Well, I think they were embarrassed. They didn't want to tell what their parents did."

"Susan did try to speak one time, but Larry was talking too much and she didn't get a chance."

When the two reticent members were asked why they thought they didn't participate more, they said little beyond, "I don't know."

"Sometimes even when a topic is interesting some people find it harder to say how they feel or think than others do. Remember we said earlier that behavior has a lot to do with whether discussions are interesting. What could you do, as a member of a group, to help these people speak, and make things more interesting for them and perhaps for everyone?"

"Well, you could keep from talking so much yourself."

"You could ask them what they have to say."

"Can you be very specific about that? What exactly would you say to someone who wasn't talking very much?" asked Miss Lantieri.

"Do you have anything to say?"

"That's no good. They wouldn't talk then because they'd feel too embarrassed."

"You could ask them a question about their parents."

"What words would you use in that question?" asked Miss Lantieri.

"I'd say, 'What do your parents do when you do something wrong?' "

"So sometimes asking a person a question about the problem being discussed might help him to speak," said Miss Lantieri. "What else could you do?"

"You could listen when everybody is talking, instead of talking yourself."

"Sometimes I don't talk, because I know nobody wants to hear me."

"How do you know, if you don't say it!"

"Well, I feel like that, anyway."

"How people feel about what others think of their contributions is very important, isn't it. There are ways that we can help people feel more comfortable, something we will call gatekeeping. That is, we can open the gate to help people who aren't participating as much as they might want to by doing something to bring them into the discussion.

"We're going to have six *different* people in the inner circle now, and half the outer circle is going to tally in the old way, just keeping track of who talks, while the other half watches for gatekeeping. When somebody does something to help another person get in, you will write down his name or initials and next to that write down what he did."

The inner circle continued discussing punishment, and much of the conversation was similar to that of the first group, but this time there was some gatekeeping activity. For example, one child turned to another and asked, "What does your mother do?" Another said, when someone was cut off just as he seemed to want to say something, "Hold it! Rosa wants to speak." And once when two youngsters began to speak at the same time, the one who was more outspoken told the shyer one to go ahead.

When the time for this discussion was up, Miss Lantieri asked the outer circle to report on the times that people had helped others get in and then on how often people spoke. This time it was noted that everyone had spoken, although some spoke more than others.

"That's all we'll do for today," said Miss Lantieri. "We've been taping today's session, and tomorrow we're going to begin by listening to part of it and then getting into small groups so that every one can practice gatekeeping."

Lesson 5—More on Bringing Others into the Group

Miss Lantieri began this session by playing a tape recording of the last discussion of the previous day, and she asked the children to raise their hands each time they heard someone open the gate for someone else. Occasionally she stopped the tape to ask exactly how the gate had been opened, and at the conclusion of this activity she said, "I think we all have a good idea of what gatekeepers can do to help bring others into a discussion. We're going to get into groups of six today, but first let's decide on a topic from our list that would be of interest to all of us. All right—whether or not we should have homework seems like a good choice. Now, let's get into groups using our nonverbal way."

When groups had been formed and everyone was seated and ready to begin, Miss Lantieri said, "Now decide on two members to be observers. One will tally how often people speak while the other will tally how often people act as gatekeepers to bring others in. We'll discuss for about five minutes, and I'll ring this bell when time is up. Then each observer will share what he found with his group. After that, if anyone else in the groups wants to comment, he can."

Miss Lantieri circulated among the groups, and after time spent sharing results within the small groups there was a total class discussion about what had happened.

Then the class selected another topic and different observers and went through the same procedure, followed again by a total group discussion and a review of some of the ways that people could be drawn into discussions.

At the conclusion of this lesson Miss Lantieri said, "We've seen that some people speak more than others even when the topic is interesting to everyone, and that's all right. We don't have to have everyone speak an equal amount of time, but it's important to give everyone an opportunity. I'd like you to notice that we didn't have any chairmen or discussion leaders, and we didn't need to, really, because everyone took some responsibility to participate and to help others participate. This is important in group discussions—that we don't simply rely on a leader to keep things going, even when we have one, but that everyone take responsibility. Next time we'll do some more with small group discussions and we'll have observers again."

Lesson 6—Using Data To Analyze
What Happens in a Group

The class briefly reviewed what they had learned about the importance of the topic being interesting and of people participating. Then they worked in groups of six, with four students discussing and two observing. One observer put a mark beside each person's initials each time he spoke, and the other observer kept track of gatekeeping. Each group chose its own topic, talked for about ten minutes, and then the observers took turns telling the entire class what happened in their groups.

The observers from group 1 reported that in their group there had been lots of gatekeeping, but only half the group spoke. When asked what they thought had caused this, the class said that it must have been the topic. The group itself reported that they had argued about the topic, and when they finally got going the two who didn't want that topic were so angry they didn't want to talk. The others tried to gatekeep but without results.

Groups 2 and 3 reported that everyone spoke and that there was some gatekeeping, and the class gave some hunches on who they thought had done what. Someone in group 3 had ten tallies for speaking and someone else had two, so the class thought the person with the ten tallies must have tried to bring in the person with the two tallies, and the observers said that this had happened. When asked whether or not they thought the topics were interesting in these two groups, the class said they thought they had been, and the groups agreed with this.

The fourth group reported that one person hadn't spoken at all, one person had spoken once, another person had spoken many times, and there was little gatekeeping. The class thought a certain child had been the one to speak a great deal, and they were right. They also concluded that the other members didn't help, because they didn't try to get in themselves or help others get in.

The group under discussion agreed, and the child who spoke the most said, "Yeah, I talked too much. The topic was interesting, and I like to talk, so I kept talking. And I wasn't sure if the other kids wanted to talk, because they didn't."

The teacher asked what he could have done to find out whether this was so, and he responded that he could have asked. Then Miss Lantieri asked the rest of the group what they might have done to improve the discussion, and they thought that they could have told the big talker in a nice way that he was speaking too much for them to get in.

"We're saying that in order for people to participate well, not only should the topic be interesting and shy people be helped to come in but people who speak easily and often should be reminded sometimes that they need to give others a turn, and both kinds of speakers should make some effort to get in or drop out on their own. That is, shy people should begin to try to get in sometimes without help and big talkers should try sometimes to be quiet and help others speak," concluded Miss Lantieri.

Lesson 7—Feeling Left Out of the Group

"Now today," said Miss Lantieri, "we're going to talk about some other reasons why some people don't participate well in a discussion, besides the things we've said so far. What are some other reasons?"

Everything mentioned by the children as possible reasons had to do with the topic, so Miss Lantieri said, "Okay, the topic is certainly important, but suppose that the topic was interesting to everyone and some people still didn't talk, and it wasn't just because some people were shy or others talked too much."

This didn't bring much response, and finally Miss Lantieri asked, "Well, can you think of a time when you were in a group, but you didn't really feel as though you were part of the group?"

Then the examples came rapidly. "One time I was in the playground and I was with a bunch of kids during lunchtime, and then they started to play punchball, and I didn't feel like part of the group anymore, because I didn't think either side wanted me on their team."

"Sometimes I don't feel like part of the group in my family. Well, like I'm the black sheep, and if somebody doesn't know what that means, well, it means that your family doesn't care what you think, and I feel that way a lot in my family."

"I was visiting at my friend's house once and there were four of us, and they decided to go to the movies and I called my mother, but she wouldn't let me go. The other kids went anyway, so I really felt out of the group then."

After more examples, Miss Lantieri said, "So it seems that we sometimes feel left out because we think others don't want us. There are many reasons for feeling left out, and people often don't participate well when they feel unwanted.

"We're going to do a little exercise now to see how it feels to want to be a part of a group but be left out. I need six people to form a group in the inner circle, so will you six people do that. Now you, Glenna, are going to be left out—that is, no one will speak to you, look at you, or listen to you. You can talk or do anything you want—but no one will pay any attention to you. For a topic, let's talk about what happened this morning when I had my preparation period and some people acted up in class, and the whole class was punished by the relief teacher."

The group talked eagerly about what had happened that day, since it was an important happening, and they managed to do a good job of cutting Glenna out. She tried to get in a number of times and finally fell silent.

"How did you feel during that session, Glenna?" asked Miss Lantieri after the discussion time was up.

"Well, I didn't feel good. I felt like nobody liked me."

"Why didn't you keep trying to get in?"

"There wasn't any point. If nobody listens, what's the use of talking?"

"Let's just take a moment now for the rest of the inner circle group to show Glenna, without words, how they *really* feel about her. Why don't you stand in the center, Glenna, and anyone who wants can come up and show you how they feel— just show, with no talking."

Four group members came up to Glenna and either shook her hand, patted her shoulder, or put an arm around her. "How do you feel now?" asked Miss Lantieri, when everyone who wanted to had had a turn.

"Much better. I feel like they like me—at least some of the people do."

"Now, let's get into groups of three and everyone will have a turn either to be left out or to leave someone out. As soon as you're ready I'll come around and say which person will be left out by the other two. We'll continue the same discussion, and we'll only do this once."

When this had been completed and discussed by the entire class, Miss Lantieri said, "Now this was an exercise in which we were specifically asked to exclude people; to leave them out. But let's think for a minute about why people sometimes don't want others to be part of their group."

"Well, sometimes you don't want somebody because you don't like them."

"Some people are show-offs, or bossy, and who wants them!"

"Sometimes you're talking about something and it isn't any of the other person's business."

"Okay, those are examples of why some people are excluded. How about how *you* feel when you're the one who's left out?"

"I don't feel good when I'm left out. It's a bad feeling."

"I don't like to be alone. I want to be with other people, so I don't like it when I'm left out."

"It makes me mad if I'm left out. I think there must be something wrong with me."

"I get mad when I'm left out, too. But I don't really care anyway."

"My feelings are hurt a lot if I think people don't want me."

"Well, we're finding out that there are a number of reasons for people being excluded. It might be the way they act, or things they say. And we also know that when this happens to us, we feel hurt, usually. So it will be good to learn how to keep from being left out when we don't want to be and how to help other people behave in ways that will keep them from being left out when they are members of groups with us. What do you do, usually, when you're part of a group and somebody does something that you don't like?"

"Well, we get mad at each other."

"I talk back to the person."

"If the other kids don't like him either, then we get rid of him."

"Well, if nobody wants the person, then he usually knows it, and he leaves by himself."

"So there are a number of ways of making people feel as if they aren't part of the group. What could we do in a situation where we don't like what somebody is doing, but we want to help the person change rather than kick him out? In other words, what can we do to help ourselves and other kids change so that we participate better in groups and don't get left out?"

"Well, you could say in a nice way how you feel."

"You could make believe you don't see what somebody is doing, if they are being a pest."

"You could tell him that if he doesn't stop what he's doing, you're going to kick him out."

"I hear several people saying that it might help a person be a better group member if he knows how the group feels about him—if he gets some feedback from other people. Sometimes people might not know why the group is annoyed, and if they know, then they can have the chance to change, if they want to. Anyway, it's clear that feelings are important, and I'm going to encourage you to say how you feel very often this year. I'll ask you how you feel about things that happen to you, or things that you're doing, and also how you feel about what other people are saying or doing. If we can say our feelings honestly, I think this will help us deal with left-out feelings —whether they're ours or other people's. When we talk about feelings it won't be to put ourselves or anyone else on the spot in embarrassing ways, but will be part of getting to know ourselves and other class members better, so we can work together."

Lessons 8 and 9—Looking at Group Membership Roles

"We've been concentrating on ways of helping people get into discussions, and I think we've learned a lot about that, because I see during the day that people are remembering to use the ideas we've been talking about. Today we're going to start by looking at these rexographed sheets about three different kinds of group behavior, called work behavior, helping behavior, and troublesome behavior. Let's take some time to read these over." (See Table 3.)

TABLE 3

Some Things People Can Do in Group Discussions[a]

work behavior	1. Have new ideas or suggestions
	2. Ask for or give information
	3. Help to explain better
	4. Pull ideas together
	5. Find out if group is ready to decide what to do
helping behavior	1. Help people get together
	2. Bring other people in
	3. Show interest and kindness
	4. Be willing to change own ideas to help group
	5. Tell others in good ways how they are behaving
troublesome behavior	1. Attack other people
	2. Not go along with other people's suggestions
	3. Talk too much
	4. Keep people from discussing, because don't like arguments
	5. Show that they do care about what's happening

[a] See Chapter 3, pp. 45–52.

The class read over the sheet and discussed it, giving examples of the different behaviors. Then Miss Lantieri asked eight people to be in the inner circle while the outer circle was divided into three segments—one to observe and tally work behavior, one to watch for helping behavior, and the third to concentrate on troublesome behavior. The inner group held a discussion for about ten minutes, received feedback for five or ten minutes, and then continued the discussion for about ten minutes more and received feedback again.

This was repeated with another group in the inner circle. Topics were selected that required trying to come to some kind of decision, for example, "Where shall we go on our next trip?" and the same topic was kept for both rounds—that is, it was continued after the feedback session. The reasons for picking a topic which involves decision-making is that the behaviors listed in Table 3 are particularly applicable to working on a specific task.

During lesson 9, Miss Lantieri had some of the behaviors written on signs, and these were placed in front of certain children, who were then expected to evidence this behavior (see "Behavior by the Label," p. 50). This was done in the inner circle with several groups having a try. Regular discussion followed in small groups, without using signs, but pupils were encouraged to try a new behavior which would be helpful and to notice the behavior of others. As with all the activities in this unit, these behaviors were observed and discussed in other areas of the curriculum.

Lesson 10—Listening Skills

"One thing that's very important in discussions is listening, and today we're going to practice listening! The way we'll practice is by repeating what we've heard, to show that we really heard it. What we're going to do is this: the first person will say how many brothers and sisters he has, and the second person will repeat what the first person said, and then tell how many brothers and sisters he has. The third person will tell *only* what the person right before him—the second person—said, and then tell how many brothers and sisters he has. Okay?"

The exercise started, and while it seemed easy, a number of youngsters had considerable difficulty with it, both because they could not remember and because they started to tell how many siblings they had before repeating what the previous person had said. When a child was wrong, the previous speaker held up his finger, and the teacher asked if anyone else could repeat. Then the one who missed had another turn. There was so much stumbling that finally the teacher said, "Let's see if we can get through five people in a row without a mistake, and instead of going in any kind of order, we'll let people raise their hands if they think they can do it." This was done until everyone had a turn.

"That was certainly harder than we thought," said Miss Lantieri. "Let's try another one, and see how we do. This time we'll take, 'On Saturdays, I like to _____,' and use the same system we started with the first time—going around rather than raising hands."

The class did much better with this round, and Miss Lantieri closed the session by saying that the next activity would also involve listening and repeating, but with people talking a little longer and with repeaters not having to say in exact words what they had heard, but just giving the general idea.

Lesson 11—More on Listening

"Today we're going to try some more listening exercises, but remember that I said we would talk for a little longer—so it will be harder. And also, we won't repeat exactly what the person before us said; we'll just give the essence, or the main idea. The topic will be, 'The most embarrassing thing that ever happened to me in school,' and those who want to participate will raise their hands. Who wants to start?"

The youngsters did quite well with this, saying, for example, "Well, you said that the most embarrassing thing that ever happened to you was the time you got a bad mark and everybody saw it. The most embarrassing thing that ever happened to me was the time when we had this play in the second grade. I still remember it—I was supposed to come out and hand another kid a message and say something. But I tripped and fell down in front of everybody, and then I forgot what to say, and some people were giggling, so I started to cry, right on the stage."

"You said that the most embarrassing thing for you was the time you fell down on the stage and started to cry; and the most embarrassing thing for me was the time. . . ."

Not everyone had a turn on this round, because Miss Lantieri stopped after about ten minutes and said, "All right, now that we have a good idea of how to do this, let's break into small groups and continue. First we'll let anyone who didn't have a turn tell about the most embarrassing school experience in the small group and then we'll move on to some other topics. Remember, we're just going to repeat the general idea of the person before us."

After a few minutes for finishing up with the first topic, the teacher introduced a second: "I wish that my teacher would. . . ." The class was in groups of four, and there was time for two more topics: "The funniest thing that ever happened to me" and "The best thing that ever happened to me." If some children did not have a turn on one topic, Miss Lantieri suggested they start first on the next encounter.

Lesson 12—Listening and Accepting

"Today," said Miss Lantieri, "we're going to do something a little different with listening and repeating. Instead of just repeating, we're going to try to accept what people say. This is different from just repeating, because we particularly want to show another person that we accept what he says. In other words, we use acceptance to show that we heard and understood what was said—not necessarily that we agree, but just that we accept the right of the other person to that opinion. For instance, suppose somebody says, 'I think Miss Lantieri is mean,' and you don't agree. You could still accept what that person said by saying, 'I guess you don't like her.' How about these examples—see if you can accept them. Remember, acceptance doesn't mean you necessarily agree."

Miss Lantieri had several sentences which the class practiced accepting, such as, "I don't like school," "That game isn't any fun," "No wonder everybody fights with you," and "Who cares what you say." The children needed a fair amount of practice to understand how to use acceptance, tending to say things like, "Maybe nobody cares what you say either," rather than, "I guess you don't care about what I have to say."

"What's the purpose of learning how to accept statements like these?" asked Miss Lantieri.

"Well, what you said. That people have a right to their own opinions."

"And how does acceptance show this?"

"Well, you say what they said, so they know that you heard it and you don't care."

"Not that you don't care, but that he can say what he wants."

"And there's a difference, isn't there," said Miss Lantieri. "You might care a lot about what he says, and even want to try to change his mind or argue with him. Of course, it's hardest to use acceptance when you don't agree with what someone says. Why might you try to use it when you don't agree?"

No one had much to offer on this question, so Miss Lantieri used as an example, "Suppose somebody said to me, 'I don't care what you say, I'm not going to sit down,' and I say, 'Who do you think you are! Just get into your seat and don't ever talk to me again that way!' How does the person feel about me?"

"Well, he doesn't like you."

"But you have to do that or he won't behave."

"But suppose, after he says, 'I don't care what you say, I'm not going to sit down,' I say, 'I guess you're sort of upset right now, and you're angry with me.' How do you think the person will feel then?"

"He won't be so mad at you."

"Yeah, but he might not sit down."

"Which way do you think the person would be more willing to talk the problem out with me—the first way or the second?"

"The second, because then he wouldn't be so mad."

"So one thing that accepting can do is to make people less angry, and then you can keep on talking instead of having an argument. And maybe you can work out a better solution to whatever the problem is. So we can use acceptance to keep anger down and settle arguments, as well as to let people know we have heard them and are willing to let them have their opinions even if we might not agree.

"For homework tonight I'm going to give you these rexographed sheets with some sentences on them, and you can write in ways of accepting these remarks. If any of you want to do them together, that's all right. Just put everyone's name on the paper, but let's not have more than four to a paper."

Lesson 13—Accepting Disagreement

After reviewing the previous night's homework in small groups, Miss Lantieri said, "Now we're going to practice some more acceptance while we're actually having group discussions. I'm going to give you some topics, and each group will split in half, with half taking the 'yes' side, and half taking the 'no' side. First we'll have a sample group in the inner circle so we can be sure of how to do it. We're going to try to accept statements whenever we think it's appropriate during a discussion that is, in a way, an argument. Who'd like to volunteer for this?"

The inner circle had as its topic, "If one child is bad in gym, then the entire class should not be allowed to go to gym," and the outer circles tallied examples of acceptance while half the inner group argued for and half against. After a feedback session the class divided into groups and worked on these topics: "Schools shouldn't give out report cards," "A good teacher wouldn't give homework," and "School usually isn't much fun." There were observers for purposes of feedback and a brief discussion took place at the close of the session.

Lesson 14—A Group Meeting

"Today we're going to have what we'll call a group meeting, to talk over the problem that came up about the way some people were working in the creative writing groups. Let's get into a circle, as we usually do, but this time you will participate only if you want to, which is different from what we have been doing. I hope that everyone will participate in group meetings, but if people don't want to, that's all right. However, if you don't join in, you have to work quietly by yourself, because talking will interfere with the rest of us. If you decide to drop out during the meeting, you can do so by very quietly going back to your place, and if you decide to come in later on, you can join us in a way that doesn't disturb anyone."

(Miss Lantieri always made group meetings optional. Sometimes topics were rather personal, or sometimes members simply weren't interested, and she felt that participation should be up to the individuals in the class. Most children participated most of the time; dropouts tended to be the two or three youngsters who caused the most difficulty in the classroom, and they sometimes didn't attend because they didn't want to be the focus of attention which would be critical of them. However, these youngsters also attended much of the time and could move in and out at will. Since Miss Lantieri also had individual conferences and small-group conferences, youngsters' problems were dealt with in a variety of ways.)

"We'll have just a few rules," continued Miss Lantieri, "which we worked out last year and which seemed pretty successful. Whenever we have these meetings, which might be whenever something comes up that needs our attention, or might be at set times, we'll have one person act as observer. This person will ring the bell whenever a subgroup of people who are talking among themselves forms or when somebody does something disruptive or disturbing which makes it hard to hear. If the bell rings four times, the meeting is over. This might not sound fair, but last year we found that it was better to end the meeting if people weren't cooperating than try to continue and hope that things would get better. Anyway, let's start with these rules and make changes as they're needed.

"Now, who has something to say about the problem of how people are working in groups?"

"I do. I was in the group with Gary this morning when we had creative writing, and he spoiled our whole group—acting silly and stuff."

"I was in that group too, and we never could do anything because of him!"

"You both seem to feel pretty angry at Gary," said Miss Lantieri.

"Of course! Who wants to be in a group with somebody who just ruins everything!"

"How do you feel about what they're saying, Gary?" asked Miss Lantieri.

"I don't know."

"Oh, he doesn't even care!"

"Let me talk! If everybody's mad at me, well, then I don't feel so good."

"Do you know why you did things that the others felt were disturbing to the group?" asked Miss Lantieri.

"I just wanted to have some fun, that's all."

"Well, *he* might think. . . ."

"Can you tell Gary directly what you're going to say," interrupted Miss Lantieri.

"Well," repeated the youngster, looking at Gary, "*you* might think that what you were doing was fun, but the rest of us didn't have any fun! And when it was time to share our ideas, we didn't even have anything, because of you."

"Did any of you in that group tell Gary how you felt?"

"Yeah, we kept telling him to stop what he was doing."

"Is that the same as telling your feelings?"

"Well, we didn't tell him how we felt, but we told him to cut it out."

"Why do you think Gary said he wanted to have some fun, and the rest of the group didn't think what he was doing was fun?" asked Miss Lantieri. "See if you can explain to Gary directly."

"You were giggling and making jokes, so maybe you thought that was fun. But nobody else in our group wanted to do that, so it wasn't fun for us."

"Do you hear what he's saying, Gary?" asked Miss Lantieri.

"Yes. He's saying, I mean, *you're* saying that I was laughing and everything, but the other kids wanted to do the assignment, so they didn't have any fun."

"And I think another group had a problem something like this," said Miss Lanticri.

"Yeah, our group did. We wanted to do the work, but Quentin didn't, so he, I mean *you,* spoiled it for the rest of us."

"Well, how did the people in the groups feel about having their talk interfered with?"

"We felt mad," was the general opinion.

"Is that what you wanted to accomplish, Gary and Quintin?"

"No, we just wanted to have some fun, that's all."

"What could you have done differently so everyone would have been happier?"

"Well we could have not been silly."

"We could have saved the fooling around for later."

"Now, what are we going to do when people fool around in work groups? Some people wanted to have fun during creative writing, which to them meant fooling around, and others wanted to finish the assignment. We've done quite a bit of work in groups already, and we know we're going to be doing a lot more. There are certain behaviors that are sort of required when we work in groups, if we're going to *do* the work. I can't be in every group, so you'll have to be able to work well without me. Fooling around *is* interfering in the group, but what can we do about people who don't want to go along?"

"Well, we should just kick them out. Let them work by themselves."

"Yeah, just have those people work by themselves. Then they won't bother anybody."

"That's the best thing."

"Will they miss anything by not working in the group?" asked Miss Lantieri.

"They could have the same assignments, so it wouldn't matter."

"The thing they miss is they don't work with other people."

"And does that matter?" asked Miss Lantieri.

"Well, we said that working in groups was good, because you can *learn* how to do it. So if you don't go with a group you won't learn that."

"Would they miss anything in the *assignment,* in creative writing, for example?"

"Yeah—they won't have the ideas from other people."

"But if they ruin it for everybody else, then that's not fair, even if they do miss something!"

"All right, now we've said that if we have people work by themselves for creative writing they miss out on learning how to work well with other people, and also they won't have a chance to share in hearing other people's ideas or adding ideas of their own. On the other hand, it's not fair to have a group spoiled by people who interfere and fool around, and since we don't have a special place to go for fooling around, and also because the assignments *are* to help us learn, sometimes people might just have to leave the group and work by themselves. How will we decide when these times are, and what will we do to move a person out of a group?"

"First, we should give the kids a chance to stay with the group and tell them to stop what they're doing."

"And we could tell them what they're doing that's not so good, and how we feel. But then, if they keep doing it, they should have to work by themselves."

That seemed to be an agreeable solution, and it was decided that if someone was too much of a cut-up, then others would raise their hands and tell Miss Lantieri that he wasn't wanted in the group anymore. This did happen, on occasion, and the child then worked by himself. During creative writing this meant that he selected a topic from the creative writing box, which was always available in the classroom, and wrote a composition on his own, joining the total group for the sharing period.

A Typical Creative Writing Lesson

Since the group meeting just described mentions creative writing, it seems appropriate to describe such a lesson. At the beginning of the year, before dividing the class into small groups for writing, Miss Lantieri scheduled creative writing activities which used the inner and outer circle, so that everyone could observe a group in action. The use of the inner circle is helpful for beginning group work of any kind, especially with children who have not had much experience in working in small groups without teacher direction. Usually the teacher should participate in the inner group, at least for the first few times. The activity to be described here has the children working in a number of small groups, but the same lesson could be carried out with a few children in the inner circle and the rest of the class observing.

Miss Lantieri set the stage for this lesson by telling this story: "Last night, when it was time for dismissal, Joey decided that he was going to hide in the coat closet, to see how long it would be before we missed him. Everyone got into line and left, except Joey, who was hiding in the closet. 'I wonder if they'll miss me by the time they get to the first landing,' Joey

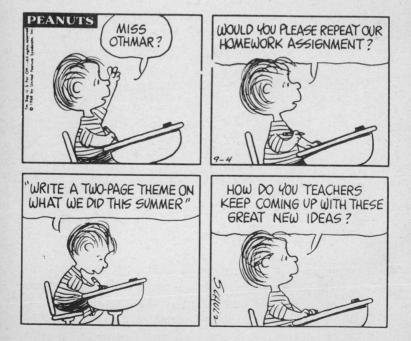

thought, 'or whether it will be when they get to the front door, or when.' Then he heard some voices and said to himself, 'Oh— here they are, already.' But when he peered out of the closet he didn't see a soul. The voices became louder, and finally he realized that the desks were talking to each other! 'Wow! They'll never believe me when I tell them about this,' he thought. Just then he spotted the tape recorder and decided that if he turned it on he'd have proof, so he did exactly that and taped what the desks said.

"Now your assignment is to write down your idea about what the desks might have been saying. We'll work in groups of four, and first we'll brainstorm and have one person act as recorder to jot everything down. Remember, when you brainstorm, every idea is acceptable."

After about ten minutes of this, the six recorders read the ideas their groups had generated, and then each person wrote his story individually, calling upon any of the ideas he had heard or using new ideas. The children continued to sit in the small groups during the writing, and the lists of ideas circulated quietly around the room for anyone's reference.

When most people had finished (those who finished early could do a number of other things while they waited), the small groups read their stories to each other and decided upon one that would be shared with the entire group. Then the class came together in a circle and listened to the six stories which had been selected and had some time for discussion of the entire activity.

More on Group Meetings

After the unit that led up to what Miss Lantieri called group meetings, these encounters were held frequently, both at scheduled times and when problems arose which seemed to need immediate attention. As time went on, Miss Lantieri was able to ask of some problems, "Can that wait until our group meeting?" which might be scheduled later in the day or in the next day or two, and the children would decide whether or not the matter needed immediate attention.

In addition, the youngsters began to deal with many of their problems in small group meetings, held during free time. Two or three or more children would gather to discuss matters of concern and attempt a resolution among themselves. At other times a few pupils would specifically ask for a meeting with Miss Lantieri about a problem which involved just their small group, and this was arranged, sometimes during the teacher's preparation period or sometimes when a special teacher was working with the rest of the class. For example, one such meeting involved five children, the paraprofessional, and Miss Lantieri and was held while the rest of the class went to gym. Three of the children involved felt that the paraprofessional, who was well liked by the class, had some favorites to whom she gave special attention, including the other two children present. Another problem-solving method employed by Miss Lantieri, at times was to ask two people involved in an argument to go out into the hall with a third child as an impartial observer and conciliator, to attempt a reconciliation.

Initially, the group meetings tended to deal with problems that arose in other areas of the children's school lives, for example, around their work with other teachers, their behavior in assembly programs, problems arising from a cross-age tutoring program they had once a week with a second grade class, and so on. It took a while before strictly personal problems were brought to the meeting. At first, the group seemed to feel that these kinds of issues would not be of interest to the entire group, but then they began to see these encounters as a time when they could bring up personal problems and receive help from the group. (Each teacher, of course, needs to decide for himself what kinds of topics he feels comfortable in dealing with in his own class.)

Some other matters which were discussed in group meetings had to do, for example, with a student teacher who was seen by the class as overly critical, another student teacher whom they considered boring, and a special teacher whom they felt was too punitive. These problems were always discussed with only Miss Lantieri present before the other adults involved were invited to participate. The special teacher who was felt by the class to be punitive attended a class meeting called for the purpose of discussing this matter and became defensive. Whenever anyone told her how he felt, she responded that that person deserved what he got, because his own behavior had brought it on. Miss Lantieri assured her that she had not been invited to be put upon the witness stand, but rather to hear the feelings of the class members and to share her own feelings, if she cared to. This resulted in the special teacher telling of the problems she faced as a new teacher and of how she often became angry because she was upset when things went wrong. The air was cleared enough on both sides to enable all participants to make a new start.

At times group meetings were called for special purposes and the topic was clear in advance. At other times when meetings were scheduled, Miss Lantieri began by asking, "Does anyone have anything to bring up?" or, "How shall we spend our time during this meeting?" If nothing particular emerged, then Miss Lantieri would ask if the class wanted to try some things she had in mind—the sorts of activities presented in Chapter 2. The group engaged in a large number of these activities. At various times they lined themselves up according to certain dimensions, such as how well they thought they did as group members, how well they thought they got along with others, or how effectively they thought they dealt with their feelings of anger. In this sort of action sociogram, the participants are asked to line themselves up from most to least according to the dimension. This activity can involve everyone or a part of the group. Often in an action sociogram a participant is permitted to move someone else, if he feels he belongs in a different place, and if a person is moved by two persons to the same spot, he is expected to stay there. Obviously, the children have to take these activities seriously, the atmosphere has to be open and accepting, and the most important part of the activities is the ensuing discussion of what happened and what feelings resulted.

Often activities which Miss Lantieri introduced grew out

of relevant group discussion, such as having children stand in the center so that others could show how they felt about them without words—a particularly appropriate approach when someone feels unwanted or disliked. At other times different children might sit in a chair in the center of the circle while other group members told how they felt about him. These were always optional activities, and while they usually grew out of things that happened in the group discussion revolving around certain individuals, anyone else not directly involved who wanted to could go into the center either for verbal or nonverbal feedback. Sometimes when apparent hostility was a problem between two people and words weren't getting anywhere, Miss Lantieri would suggest that they face each other and clasp hands and push against each other. They would then discuss their feelings about what happened, which often led to a recognition of feelings which did not come out of the talk alone. At other times they would discuss certain opening sentences like, "What I like about myself," "What I don't like about myself," "If I had only twenty four hours left to live, I'd spend it. . . ." Very often Miss Lantieri would act as a model, telling personal feelings or events from her own life in order to legitimize an openness of sharing in the group.

Bringing about a Change in Circumstances— A Group Meeting

A major purpose of these encounters was to bring about change, not only in the children but in their circumstances. Early in the year the youngsters had a problem of circumstance, which a group meeting helped them to resolve; and they learned that they *could* effect change in their lives.

One of their special teachers was covering material they had had before, and so they weren't interested in the content. In addition, they went to this class directly after the weekly assembly program, where they had been sitting for a long time, and they became restless. The result was that they misbehaved, and this came up at a group meeting, when they said that they were "bad" again with Miss X. They discussed the reasons for this, and while some children felt that perhaps they needed the review and that they should give the teacher more of a chance, others insisted that since they had already gone to this class three times, it was obvious that the teacher was not just review-ing—this *was* the content. Everyone agreed that they needed a five-minute break after the assembly, as they often had in their own class. The group decided that this teacher should know how they felt and suggested that Miss Lantieri tell her. Then they decided that they should tell her themselves, but they were worried that they wouldn't know how to do it and also that the teacher would think they didn't like her, which was not the case.

Miss Lantieri asked, "If you *were* going to tell her, what would you say? Let's imagine that we send a person to talk to her, and let's have one person play that part and another play the part of Miss X." This was the first time during the year that the class engaged in role-playing, a device frequently used by Miss Lantieri.

Two people volunteered to play the part of pupil and teacher, and the pupil pretended that he had gone to have a conference with Miss X. "Good morning, Miss X," he began. "We've been talking about the problem that we have in your class, and we decided that we don't behave, because—well, we're bored. We've already learned about the stuff you're teaching us."

The pupil playing the part of Miss X replied, "Well, what do you think would be more interesting?"

"I don't know, but we could ask the rest of the class. And another thing is that when we come to your class we've just been to assembly, and we wondered if we could have a five-minute break. We do that in our own class, and we just talk and stuff, and when Miss Lantieri flicks the light we all go back to our seats and get quiet."

When the role-playing had finished, the class listened to the tape of what had happened (Miss Lantieri usually taped group meetings), and one child had the idea that Miss X should listen to the tape of the whole meeting. Everyone agreed that that would be a good idea, and Miss Lantieri approached

Miss X, who was most amenable and thought enough of what she heard to begin her next class session with the fifth graders by saying she had heard the tape, that she was certainly willing to start the class with a five-minute break, and that she would like to talk about another unit of study with them. This discussion was held and the unit was changed.

This entire episode meant a great deal to the class, because it helped them to realize that they could make changes in their circumstances. Often when faced with situations that brought on "what's the use" feelings, they would remind themselves of this early experience with Miss X, and this encouraged them to go on with whatever they were attempting to do.

Chairs as Status Symbols—A Group Meeting

Another encounter of particular interest had to do with chairs. Each month the children changed seats according to some dimension like sitting next to a good friend or next to someone who wasn't well known or boys next to girls or randomly by selecting names from a box. The classroom was equipped with rectangular double desks which could be joined in any combination, plus six single desks, which also could be placed next to other desks or kept apart, as the occupant wished; most children wanted at least one turn at a single desk. Although there was much moving around during the day for various activities, there was a kind of home base set-up which was more or less permanent for the month and which might be a circle, a semicircle, or various other groupings. Each month Miss Lantieri talked with the class about some of the things they would be doing, and then they would decide on the basic arrangement which would be most appropriate. The teacher then drew this arrangement in diagram form on the board, each place was assigned a number, and the youngsters selected the numbers they wanted. Naturally, this involved some compromising. If, for example, seven youngsters wanted the six single desks and could not come to any quick solution, Miss Lantieri might ask the seven to go outside for a few moments and settle it among themselves. The group meeting described next occurred on a day when a seating change had been made.

The meeting began with some discussion of the difficult day had by Doreen, who had been reported for misbehavior in the library, refused to do her work during the day, and was obviously angry. She was a child who was usually very cooperative, and when asked what had happened she didn't have much to say.

"I know you wanted a single desk," said Miss Lantieri, "and you didn't get one."

"That's not the reason," said another child. "It's because she lost her big chair."

"Yeah, I got her old place, and so I got the big chair, and that's why she's mad," said Lois.

Some further discussion revealed that Lois had also jeered at Doreen saying, "Ha, ha, you think you're so smart, but I got the good chair!"

"I guess the big chair was pretty important to you," said Miss Lantieri. "How many others would want a big chair if they could have one?"

The entire class raised their hands, and so began an exploration of the subject of the big chairs. There were four big chairs in the classroom in addition to the teacher's chair, and these chairs were special to the children, though the teacher had been unaware of this. Some of these chairs were switched when seats were switched, but one child, with whom the others were not likely to tangle, kept his large chair for the entire year and even had his name on it.

"What is it about a big chair that makes it desirable?" asked Miss Lantieri.

"Well, it's just better."

"It's like a teacher's chair."

"It makes you feel more important because it's big."

"If you have a big chair it's easier to tell which one is yours."

"And why does that matter?" asked the teacher.

"Well, it's not so bad this year, but sometimes other kids

use your chair and they get it all inky and stuff. If you have a big chair, well, it's easier to keep track of."

"Anyway, it's better to have your own chair all the time."

"But we move around so much in our room that everybody's always in somebody else's chair. Does that bother you?" asked Miss Lantieri.

"Yes. We should keep our own chairs."

"You know, this is all a complete surprise to me," said Miss Lantieri. "I didn't even know that anybody cared about the chairs, and I didn't know that there was anything special about the big chairs. Which just shows that if things aren't talked about, some things that are important will never be known. Now, what about all this moving around. Should we carry our own chairs with us all the time?"

There was a good deal of discussion about this, and they finally decided that it would be impractical to carry a chair every time they moved. Some children said that the big chairs should go to the big children while others thought they should go to the small children so they could see better. No decisions were reached other than that they wouldn't carry their chairs with them each time they moved during the day.

About twenty minutes after the meeting ended, Doreen left the room for a few minutes, and Lois, the child who had taken the big chair away from her, said, "I've got an idea. Let's play a trick on Doreen and switch the chairs!" She quickly put the big chair back at Doreen's place and then everyone waited expectantly. When Doreen came back and sat down, she felt the chair and then looked around and said, "Wait a minute!" and everyone laughed together. Then she took the chair back to Lois and said, "You need the chair more than I do, because you're bigger," and they made an exchange, and everybody seemed pleased.

The big chairs were still considered desirable, but talking out the whole matter was enough to prevent further conflict about their ownership. Much of the time the big chairs ended up at a round table in back of the room which was taller than the desks, and the chairs often stayed there because no one cared enough about them to bother retrieving them. Thus, the episode of the chairs was resolved.

My Sister Is a Pest—A Group Meeting

Sometimes children brought up problems at the group meetings which they faced at home, and one day a child began talking about the trouble he was having with a younger sister who was in prekindergarten. He talked about the fact that his sister always pestered him and tattled on him to his mother, making things up about him which he had not done and doing naughty things herself which she denied. His mother always believed his sister rather than him, and he was very discouraged about the whole situation. Some class members suggested to him that he keep a record of his sister's behavior, writing down what she did, and then show it to his mother. (This suggestion probably arose from the tallying activities in the unit on communication, and also because Miss Lantieri often used tallying in the beginning of the year to help change the behavior of people who called out and interrupted. She would give someone a card on which to record the number of times children called out during discussion when it was not their turn. The record was shown to those who had called out—usually to the amazement of the people whose behavior had been checked, since they usually did not realize they were interrupting so often. The children accepted the objective record of their behavior very well since it was presented as, "You probably didn't realize how many times you called out," and they worked on changing their behavior. After the child who kept the tallies had spoken with those who called out, he would turn the card in to Miss Lantieri and the total class was not involved.)

The youngster who told of his problems with his mother and sister accepted the class suggestion to keep a record and then showed this document to his mother. A few days later when his mother came to school to pick up his younger sister, she dropped in to see Miss Lantieri to find out how her boy was doing (he was a child with many problems) and she mentioned the list he had kept of his sister's behavior. She said that at first she didn't believe him and thought he had made it all up, but then she decided he couldn't possibly have invented all those things. She began to observe the behavior of both children and found that much of what he said was true and that she did favor the little girl. One result of this action on her son's part was that instead of expecting him to take care of his little sister in the afternoons (the mother left for work as soon as the son returned from school, and he cared for his sister until his father came home at dinner time), she hired a baby-sitter and permitted her son to attend the after-school center, which is what he wanted to do.

The Teacher as Target in Group Meetings

In a classroom which has an open and accepting environment, the teacher must be willing to come under attack and listen and attempt to change, just as the children do. Two examples of youngsters telling Miss Lantieri of their annoyance with her are presented here.

At several group meetings the children talked about their behavior during assembly programs, when they often fooled around if the programs were boring to them. Miss Lantieri never was able to do much besides sympathize with them, because she usually felt that the assembly was boring when they did, yet attendance was mandatory. They all understood that there were occasions such as assembly time when their noise interfered with others and should be curtailed, but it was still difficult for them to sit quietly. The school faculty was working on making the programs more interesting, but it was not always possible to tell in advance whether a program would be worthwhile.

After one assembly program, all the fifth grade teachers were spoken to about the noise their classes had made, and the next time many teachers had their children leave an empty seat between occupied seats to prevent talking. Miss Lantieri asked all the boys to leave empty spaces, but the girls could sit next to one another. The boys were furious, and during the next group meeting they said that what she had done was unfair and that it showed she didn't trust any boys, no matter that they were like, and trusted all the girls. She accepted their anger and told them that the fifth grade teachers had been reprimanded about the noises their classes had made. Then the children wanted to know why she had not spoken to them at the time they were noisy, and Miss Lantieri said she hadn't wanted to scold them because she too felt that the program was poor. After more talk, they decided that the next time they would not skip seats and would try to be quiet; at the next assembly program they were the only class sitting all together, which made them so proud they managed to be quiet. After that, some people sat by themselves when they knew they were going to talk, and this became a kind of solution. However, the reason for telling of this episode is to indicate that the children knew they could air their grievances about their teacher directly with her.

Another time when some of the children let Miss Lantieri know of their displeasure with her was at report card time. Several children had received "improving" when they had expected "satisfactory," and they were very upset about this. They felt that they had been inadequately prepared for these grades and thus had not prepared their parents, which meant that the results for them were going to be most unpleasant. "How could you do this to me," asked one child, "when you know what things are like at my house?" Miss Lantieri accepted their feelings of anger and realized that she *had not* adequately shared with them her evaluation of their work. The group talked about what should be done in the future to prevent this kind of situation from occurring.

The encounters described in this chapter are not presented as a solution to all the many classroom problems which teachers and children face. In this particular class, where many of the children had trying home situations and were confronted with many problems every day, all of their difficulties were certainly not resolved, inside or outside the classroom. However, a large number of their problems were dealt with, and many were resolved. The children did learn to care about each other and help one another, and one bit of evidence for this is that there was only one physical fight in the classroom during the entire year—an unusual situation in this neighborhood even when suppression of fighting is attempted through watchful tyranny. Because the children had a teacher who cared about them and who thought it important for them to care about themselves and each other, and who arranged the classroom environment to encourage encounters which were open and caring, the children in Miss Lantieri's class learned a great deal that is all too often not included in the school curriculum.

Selected References

William Glasser. *Schools Without Failure*, New York: Harper & Row, Publishers, 1969.

those other adults:
the parent, the principal,
the paraprofessional, the peer

Teachers work closely with other adults as well as with children. Even the teacher who is in sole charge of a self-contained classroom encounters administrators, parents, and other teachers, and whether or not teaching is satisfying as a profession depends to some degree upon relations with these other adults. Sometimes problems arise in schools as adults work together—problems which may grow out of the superior-subordinate relation between supervising teacher and student teacher, between principal and teacher, or between teacher and paraprofessional. Differences can also occur among peers when teachers work together in the same classroom, share committee assignments, or simply meet socially in the teachers' lounge.

How you work with others depends very largely upon you. You can get along with the most determined battle-axe, if you want to make the effort or you can quarrel with the meekest of souls, if you care to. Just as you can *acquire* skill in working with children, you can acquire similar skill with adults. Once you own certain behaviors for working effectively with people, then it is up to you to decide how and when to use them. If, for example, you are a student teacher who feels you are not being given enough to do in your classroom, then it is your responsibility to make your feelings known to your supervisory teacher. You can say, with evident anger, "There's no point in my even being in this classroom if I can't ever get to do anything!" or you can say, "I feel as if I'm ready to take on more responsibility, and I think I have some fairly good ideas that relate to the unit we're covering. I'd like to share some of my plans with you, so you can see what you think about them and maybe give me some hints about what else I might do." It seems clear that the latter behavior is more apt to bring about the desired change in circumstances.

This chapter contains activities to help you increase your skill in working with other adults. Illustrations and skill sessions about giving and receiving help, conferencing, and negotiating are included.

Giving and Receiving Help

This section is included to help you practice some additional verbal behavior. Take a moment to look at Table 4, which will be used in tallying the behavior of a consultant as he attempts to help a client solve a problem. Most people, when someone shares a problem with them, tend to use behavior on the left-hand side of the table. That is, they suggest a solution or further define the problem or convey doubt about the client's ability to solve the problem, or interpret his feelings for him.

Table 4

A Consulting Exercise in Giving and Receiving Help

Participate in trios: an observer, a client, and a consultant. The observer will make a tally mark in the appropriate box each time the *consultant* (the helper) speaks. If the observer wants to remember certain remarks, he can jot down a few words in the margin as he tallies.

the consultant

1L *Suggests* to the client what the problem is, what the facts are, what solutions or actions will work.	IR *Asks for* further clarification of the client's perceptions of the problem, the facts involved, the situation as it exists.
2L *Tells* the client what his feelings, motivations, or inadequacies are rather than exploring these with him.	2R *Explores* with the client what his feelings, ideas, and motives are and accepts these, so that both will arrive at a clear understanding of what is involved.
3L *Conveys doubt* that the client can solve the problem.	3R *Encourages* the client to use his own abilities in dealing with and solving the problem.

However, verbal behavior such as that described on the right-hand side of the table, especially in the beginning of the consultation, may be more helpful. Certainly, if we believe that people should be helped to become more self-sufficient and self-reliant, we will want to try the kind of behavior described on the right-hand side. We will want to ask for further clarification, because we will want to understand as much as possible of the situation, and we will want to help the client determine if the problem he believes he faces is, in reality, *the* problem. We will want to explore the client's motivations and feelings *with* him rather than *for* him, and we will want to encourage him to use his own abilities in arriving at possible solutions. This does not mean that a consultant never suggests solutions or actions— merely that he gives the client as much opportunity as possible to use his own strengths in problem-solving. *Sharing* problems and *relying on someone else* to solve these problems are two quite different things. We need to learn to share problems, perhaps more than we do now, and we need to listen to and help those who share with us; but most of us do *not* need additional practice in giving advice to others or in seeking ready-made solutions from others.

Three examples of consulting sessions will be presented before you try some skill sessions of your own around the process of giving and receiving help, two in which the helpers' verbal behaviors are primarily from the left-hand side af Table 4 and one in which the consultant's talk falls primarily on the right-hand side.

Consultation 1

"I have a child in my class who is such a problem I just don't know what I'm going to do with him. He ruins everything."

"Well, that's a common problem for new teachers, but I'll tell you, if you're ever going to get anywhere you've got to crack down on this kid and let him know who's boss. That's the only thing that will work; I can tell you from bitter experience."

"Well, that's the trouble. I do crack down on him, and I feel guilty about it, because I know he has so many problems and I'm not helping him."

"Listen, you're not a psychiatrist or a magician, and you can't solve the problems of the world. Your trouble is you're too idealistic. What you think is cracking down probably is nothing. I mean, you really have to be strict! Don't let him get away with anything!"

"But he doesn't listen to me. He wanders around the room, and I tell him to sit down. I've screamed at him and threatened him with every kind of punishment I know of, but I can't make him sit in his seat, so what am I supposed to do?"

"You just can't let him get away with that. If you were stern enough he wouldn't get out of his seat in the first place!"

"Well, I guess I just don't know what to do. Anyway, it's pretty depressing."

"Just take my advice and let him know who's boss, and you'll see what a difference it will make. You'll have kids like that all the time, and it's nothing to get so upset about. Just take them in your stride like the rest of us, and don't let it get you."

Consultation 2

"I have a child in my class who is such a problem I just don't know what I'm going to do with him. He ruins everything."

"Well, dear, let's see if we can't talk about it. It's Bobby you're talking about isn't it?"

"Yes, and I just can't seem to get anywhere with him. If I try to be nice to him that doesn't work, if I yell at him that doesn't work."

"I know how difficult some of our children can be, but we really must try to have patience. After all, they have such terrible home lives, many of them, and certainly Bobby does. I think if you just try to give him a little extra love and attention things will be all right."

"But he acts up so in class and really takes so much of my time. And he calls out all the time and wanders about the room; he hits the other kids and he's just a terrible problem."

"*We* always try to say that a child *has* problems rather than that he *is* a problem. Now if you just keep trying and if you give him some extra things to do, or if you really show him that you care about him, I think things will work out eventually. We all have these problems, and I think you're just a little more upset than you need to be. Tomorrow will look brighter, I'm sure."

Consultation 3

"I have a child in my class who is such a problem I just don't know what I'm going to do with him. He ruins everything."

"You seem pretty upset. What's the trouble?"

"Well, I know that Bobby has a difficult home life, and I know he's not a happy child, but I can't seem to be patient with him, which is what I know he needs. Sometimes I can hold my temper, but much of the time I end up yelling at him, and that just makes him worse. But sometimes he's so terrible that I can't help it. Like today. We were doing math, and I think the lesson was pretty interesting. Everyone was using cuisenaire rods, which they like, and they had some worksheets with different problems on them. Well, Bobby did his for about three minutes and then he began throwing rods at people and giggling. I yelled at him and he stopped for a minute, and then he got up and began walking around, which I have told him a hundred times not to do."

"What did you do then?"

"Well, at that point he wasn't bothering anybody, so I didn't say anything. That's one of the troubles, I guess. I tell him he can't do certain things but then if he does them and it doesn't bother anybody, I let him get away with it."

"Do you care if he walks around the room?"

"No, not really, if he doesn't bother anybody."

"So you've made a sort of blanket rule for Bobby about staying in his seat, which you don't seem to feel is really important, because sometimes you don't care if he walks around. What could you do instead of having that rule?"

"Well, I suppose I could ask him to sit down when it was important, or when he's bothering people, and let him walk around when he's restless at other times, if he doesn't bother anybody."

"That sounds like a good plan. One thing that may be important is to sanction his behavior rather than ignore it. For example, if he walks around when you've asked him to sit down, it may be better to recognize this in some way, perhaps by saying, 'I guess sitting is too hard to you right now, Bobby, so it's okay if you walk around for awhile. When you're ready, sit down and I'll see if you need any help.' "

"That sounds pretty good—I'm going to try that. And another thing. I know that when I lose my temper it makes things worse, because then he becomes impossible. When I keep calm and talk to him gently, things are okay with us. I think I'm improving a little bit, because I don't seem to yell at him as much as I used to. But he takes so much of my time, sometimes, when I decide to work things through with him, that I feel guilty about the other kids."

"You seem to have given Bobby a lot of thought and attention, and it sounds as if you're at least on the way to solving things. I have one observation which might help, and that is not to be overly concerned about the time spent on helping him. If the others see that your helpful behavior has results, I think that will be one of the most important learnings they'll have—seeing that patience and understanding can work with a difficult child."

"Well that *is* a good thing to keep in mind. And besides, Bobby's behavior improves when I keep my cool. He's less disruptive, so I guess in the long run he'll take less time away from the class. Thanks for listening to me. I feel much better now—I'm even ready to move on to the next episode of 'Life with Bobby!' "

In the first two consultation sessions we saw that the talk of the consultants fell primarily on the left-hand side of Table 4, the more directive side. Although they gave different kinds of advice, it is doubtful that the client felt helped by either of them. In the third situation, the client talked more, and the consultant's verbal behavior would be tallied mainly on the right-hand, or nondirective, side. The client felt pretty good at the end of this last episode. Notice that the consultant in the third example *did* make suggestions, but first spent time getting at the client's feelings and perceptions and helped the client explore solutions. Certainly, there is nothing wrong with offering solutions or helping to clarify the problem if you as the consultant see alternatives the client does not see. Just allow plenty of time for the client to do his own exploring first. Use your expertise in helping the client clarify his problems and arrive at solutions, and offer other possibilities only when it is clear that the client is not likely to arrive at them himself. Otherwise, you are making your client dependent upon "the expert" rather than helping him to become increasingly independent.

All of us are in the role of consultant many times during the day if we are teachers, for pupils constantly come to us directly with problems or indicate in indirect ways that they have problems with which they need help. Family members and friends also bring their problems to us, so we have many opportunities to practice consulting behavior. In order to own the right-hand behavior of Table 4, you will have to practice it. As always, then you will make your own decisions about when and where, or even whether, to use it.

Skill Session 1—Giving and Receiving Help

Divide into trios in some new way and then decide within each trio who will be the consultant, who the observer, and who the client. The client may choose a personal or a professional problem to present to the consultant, but the problem should be real and should also be capable of solution.

The observer will take a blank piece of paper and divide it into six squares, using Table 4 as the model. Then, each time the *consultant* speaks, the observer will make a tally mark in the appropriate square. The time schedule should be about as follows: ten minutes for the first round of discussion and five minutes for feedback, during which the observer tells his findings, the client tells how he feels about the help he is receiving, and the consultant tells how he thinks he's doing. Then there will be another ten-minute round of consulting, so that the feedback can be used, followed again by five minutes of feedback, and then everyone should change roles. Do this until each person has had a turn to be client, consultant, and observer.

Conferencing

When conferring with another adult it is not enough to want the "right" things to happen or to have good feelings toward the other person. You need to know how to deal effectively with a wide range of expression of feelings, from hostility to concern. This book has provided you with many tools you can use during conferences, and now you will be presented with a number of role-playing situations so that you may practice using some of these tools. Some examples of conference discussions are included.

Parent-Teacher Conferences

Parents face problems rather similar to those faced by teachers, but most mothers and fathers have even fewer opportunities to learn creative and effective ways of dealing with these problems than teachers do. Teachers tend to be controlling in their behavior with students, and parents have these same tendencies with their own children; economically deprived parents are evidently even more controlling than middle class parents.[1] It is important for the teacher, who is the professionally trained person, and who, therefore, presumably has more skill and know-how than the parent, to conduct conferences in ways that are helpful and that will open up some new possibilities for parents.

Let us look in on portions of several parent conferences.

Parent–Teacher Conference 1

TEACHER: I called you in because Tommy is such a problem in class. He doesn't listen, he can't follow directions, and he annoys the other children. I just don't know what I'm going to do about him.

[1] Basil Bernstein, "Social Structure, Language and Learning," *Educational Research,* Vol. III, No. 3 (June 1961).

PARENT: Well he certainly doesn't behave this way at home! He never gives us any trouble. It must be something that you're doing here at school!

Parent–Teacher Conference 2

TEACHER: I called you in because Tommy is such a problem in class. He doesn't listen, he can't follow directions, and he annoys the other children. I just don't know what I'm going to do about him.

PARENT: Well, I can't do anything with him either! Don't expect me to solve your problems for you!

Parent–Teacher Conference 3

TEACHER: I called you in because Tommy is such a problem in class. He doesn't listen, he can't follow directions, and he annoys the other children. I just don't know what I'm going to do about him.

PARENT: All he needs is a good smack every so often, and you have my permission to give it to him whenever you want!

Parent–Teacher Conference 4

TEACHER: I'm so glad you could come in today to talk with me. I look forward to meeting the parents of children in the class, since we both know the children, but we always know them just a little differently, and, of course, parents know so much more about their children than I do. I've found that we can usually be helpful to each other. Tell me, what kinds of things does Tommy have to say about school?

PARENT: Well, he doesn't talk very much about it, to tell you the truth. I guess he likes it okay. Has he been causing any trouble?

TEACHER: Well, I don't know if I'd call it trouble, but sometimes I think he'd rather be someplace else than here in school.

PARENT: He can certainly cause trouble at home, I'll tell you. I've yelled at him until I get hoarse, and his father hits him, and we've done everything to make him behave. But he's a terrible problem.

TEACHER: Sometimes he's a problem for me too, so I know what you mean. But I've been trying to figure out how to get him interested in things so that he won't be so restless. I've noticed that when there's something that he really wants to do, he can concentrate and do a good job. For example, we were making book covers for a library display, and he got interested in how the bulletin board looked, so we put him in charge and he worked very hard on that. I was pleased and he was very proud.

PARENT: Well, that's nice. I don't hear too many nice things about Tommy, I'm afraid.

TEACHER: Anyway, after that I just decided that I was going to turn over a new leaf with Tommy, and go out of my way to help him get along better and . . .

These portions of four parent-teacher conferences were presented to give some indication of the varied responses which the opening, rather attacking, lines of the first approach evoked and to indicate with the last example a more helpful method of conferencing.

Skill Session 2—Role-Playing Parent Conferences

Divide into trios, with one person being the observer, one the parent, and one the teacher. The observer will merely watch and listen and tell the other two how he perceived them at the end of each round. Change roles after each conference so that everyone has a turn at each role. Either the parent or teacher will speak the opening lines, as indicated, and the conference will continue from there in whatever direction you take it.

Allow about five minutes for the first round, a few minutes for feedback, and then have another round of both conferencing and feedback.

CONFERENCE 1, PARENT: I'd like to know why Susan isn't in the same reading group with Mary and Billy. I know she can read as well as they can, and I don't see why she can't be in the best reading group.

CONFERENCE 2, PARENT: Well, if you did your job right, George wouldn't have to stay back. It's supposed to be your job to teach him so he'll understand.

CONFERENCE 3, PARENT: Jamey told me that you pushed him down into his chair today and hurt his arm, and I'd like to know what right you have to do that to my boy. I'm not going to put up with any brutality, you can be sure of that!

CONFERENCE 4, PARENT: Frankly, I think Wendy's problem is that she's not stimulated enough with the program here, and that's why she acts up. She's a very bright child, you know.

CONFERENCE 5, PARENT: I think the children have too much freedom in your class. They shouldn't be allowed to walk around like you let them, and they should show more respect.

CONFERENCE 6, PARENT: I just don't know what to do about Larry. He runs around with such a wild gang, and half the time I don't know where he is or what he's doing. I'm worried sick.

CONFERENCE 7, TEACHER: I need your help. Patty doesn't seem to have an easy time making friends in the class, and I don't think she's as happy as she might be. I feel that I'm not doing as much as I could for her. She's so shy and she hardly ever speaks. Perhaps you can tell me something about how she feels about school.

CONFERENCE 8, TEACHER: Brenda tells me that you aren't too pleased about our study of sex education, so I thought I'd ask you to come by so we could talk.

CONFERENCE 9, TEACHER: I asked you to come in because we've definitely made the decision to retain Alan in the same grade next year, and I wanted you to know as early as possible.

CONFERENCE 10 (For this group conference, two trios should combine, so that there are six members: one teacher, one observer, and four parents.) TEACHER: We can spend our time discussing anything we want to during this conference, but perhaps we might begin by finding out how you think your children are doing and what their reactions are to school this year.

Conferencing with Other School Adults

In this section you will be presented with some sample teacher-principal conferences and then a number of opening lines for role-playing of conferences between teachers and principals, paraprofessionals, student teachers, and peers.

Teacher–Principal Conference 1

TEACHER: I'd like to speak to you about the rule that we can't have more than two reading groups. Frankly, I think this makes the groups too large, and I can't possibly reach everyone, and I don't know why we have such a ridiculous rule!

PRINCIPAL: Well, our more experienced teachers don't seem to have any problems with this. There are reasons for not having more than two reading groups, and they have to do with discipline problems, among other things. *You* certainly don't seem to have solved your many problems in that area by any means! I think what you should do is observe in Miss Goodall's room some time this week and see how she does things. I know that you're new, and I don't expect everything to go perfectly with you, but I do expect you to at least *try* to work within our framework—which has been set up for very good reasons by people with *much* more experience than you!

Teacher–Principal Conference 2

TEACHER: I'm awfully glad you were willing to give me this time to talk with you. I appreciate it.

PRINCIPAL: Well, that's what I'm here for—to help out if I can.

TEACHER: I know I've been here only a few months and still have an enormous amount to learn, but I think I'm making some good progress. Anyway, I'm taking a course in reading at the university, and I'd like to try some of the things we're learning. The instructor has been encouraging us to be sort of innovative and try things that we believe would improve learning in our classrooms. I know that new teachers in our school are encouraged to have only two reading groups, but I thought I'd like to take the slowest kids from one group and the fastest kids from the other and make two extra groups. I think the kids would really do better that way. I have the program all mapped out here, with the names and how we'd fit everything in and what everybody would be doing for this first sample week. I'd really like to give it a try.

PRINCIPAL: Well, I suppose it's a good thing for you to be thinking about trying new things. I don't see any reason against your plan. Why don't you try it for a few weeks, anyway, and see how it goes.

(There *are* times when the best way to extend the limits in your classroom is simply to extend them—without asking or requesting; that is, just assume that you can do whatever it is you have planned, and go ahead. You will have to be the judge of what methods are available to you to bring about change.)

Skill Session 3—Role-Playing Conferences with Other Adults in the School

Continue the same system of dividing into trios, with one person serving as observer, one as teacher, and the third as the other adult involved. Change roles after each conference so that everyone has turns at each role.

Conferring with the Principal

CONFERENCE 1, PRINCIPAL: Why is it that your class always makes so much noise when they go through the halls? Can't you do anything about it?

CONFERENCE 2, PRINCIPAL: Now, I don't say that we have to stick exactly to the curriculum outline, but I'd like to hear a little bit more from you on why you have this unit on "Why Poor People Pay More."

CONFERENCE 3, PRINCIPAL: I've heard some parent complaints about the lack of regular homework in your class. Our parents like to see homework sheets or workbooks, or notebooks— things they can understand. They don't count watching a television program or interviewing a neighbor as homework.

CONFERENCE 4, PRINCIPAL: Do you think it's wise to wear clothes that so many other people think are improper attire for a teacher?

Conferring with the Paraprofessional

CONFERENCE 1, PARAPROFESSIONAL: I don't like to talk out of turn, but it seems to me that the problems in this class are because you aren't strict enough with these children.

CONFERENCE 2, PARAPROFESSIONAL: When I was hired for this job I thought I was going to do more than wash the paint jars and check the attendance!

CONFERENCE 3, TEACHER: During our meeting today I wonder if we could spend some time talking about different ways that we talk to children. I noticed that you had to spend quite a bit of time today scolding the children in your reading group. What seemed to be the trouble?

CONFERENCE 4, TEACHER: I wonder what we can do so that we don't have children asking me something and getting one answer and then going to you and getting a different answer.

Conferring with the Student Teacher

CONFERENCE 1, STUDENT TEACHER: We were taught at the college that teachers should not teach as if everyone were in the same place, the way you do. We were told to group for everything, including spelling, and to include words from a variety of sources—not just use the same spelling workbooks for everybody, as you do here.

CONFERENCE 2, STUDENT TEACHER: I don't think I'll ever be able to teach math or music. I'm so terrible in those subjects myself.

CONFERENCE 3, SUPERVISING TEACHER: I think you should be taking more initiative—moving around to help the children, stepping in when they argue, and so on. If you're going to be a teacher, you can't just sit back and move only when I tell you to.

CONFERENCE 4, SUPERVISING TEACHER: Why do you think the children are always so noisy when you're teaching?

Conferring with Peers

CONFERENCE 1, TEACHER: We have to work together in the room as partners for an entire year, but if we don't start getting along better, I'm afraid that the year isn't going to be very profitable for either of us. What's wrong between us?

CONFERENCE 2, TEACHER: You have a lot of good qualities, and I like working with you, but there are a few things I'd like to bring up. For one thing, I think your group makes too much noise when we're working at the same time. And another thing—when I tell certain kids that they can't do certain things, like go out for a drink, how come you always tell them they can go?

CONFERENCE 3, TEACHER: I'm really discouraged. This week I don't think I've had one good day. The kids are just getting more and more wild, and they don't listen to me. I think I'm going to quit before I get fired.

CONFERENCE 4 (Combine two trios for this role-play of a grade meeting and have five teachers and one observer.)

TEACHER 1: I think we ought to have some system of trading children. We all know that some kids don't get along with some teachers as well as with others, and if we trade off with each other, things might be better.

TEACHER 2: I notice that you only make that suggestion during a year when you have a lot of discipline problems you'd like to get rid of!

CONFERENCE 5 (Combine two trios for this role-play of a classroom team meeting and have five team members and one observer.)

TEACHER 1: Well, I guess I blew the science lesson that I did with the total group today. What do the rest of you think?

TEACHER 2: I agree with you, and I'm beginning to think that you say that too easily. Then the rest of us say reassuring things to you, and the next time you're unprepared again. I'm getting tired of it, frankly.

CONFERENCE 6 (Once again combine trios for this role-play of a group of teachers talking informally in the teachers' room.)

TEACHER 1: I think we should just get together and make ourselves heard. The staff meetings are a waste of time, and we ought to have more say in what goes on in the planning of them. Why don't we just go and speak to Mr. Borden?

TEACHER 2: Well, I don't know. He won't like that!

TEACHER 3: What difference does that make! The whole point is that *we* don't like the way he runs things, including the staff meetings.

Negotiating

In the following session you will have an opportunity to participate as a member of a group which will negotiate with three other groups. The four groups involved must come to a common decision even though the interests of the various groups may differ.

Skill Session 4—Who Shall Control the Project?

The federal government has designated your community as an experimental area which is to receive ten million dollars to finance a two-year project for improving the school system. The size of the system is such that ten million dollars is an enormous amount of money. There are no guidelines as to how the money is to be spent other than that four groups of citizens should be consulted, and one of these four groups must have absolute control over, and accountability for, the spending of the money. In essence, this means that the group which controls the funds controls the project.

The four groups to be consulted are defined as parents with children currently in the school system, community residents who do not necessarily have children in the system, teachers currently working in the system, and administrators currently in the system.

The negotiation session to determine who will control the funds will be conducted in the following manner:

1. Divide into four groups of approximately equal size, each group representing one of the aforementioned populations. Meet separately by groups and determine what you believe the strengths of your group to be as compared with the other groups. Take about half an hour for this session, and actually make a written list of the strengths of your group.
2. Take five minutes to elect a representative who will meet with representatives from each of the other three groups for a preliminary discussion session. This session will be held before the entire group and will last about fifteen minutes, but will *not* make any final decision about which group should take control.

3. The representatives will return to their respective groups, and each group will take about fifteen minutes to prepare for a final round of negotiations. Groups may decide to select a different negotiator, or they may keep the same person. They will also elect a floor manager who may communicate with the negotiator during the final round.

4. The negotiators will meet again before the entire group for exactly twenty minutes. This is the *absolute* time limit, and someone should act as timekeeper. Each group's floor manager may communicate with his negotiator, and negotiators may communicate with their groups, through the floor manager either orally or in writing. The negotiators *must* come to a final decision as to who will control the project by the end of the twenty-minute period.

5. Have a total group discussion period to deal with the thoughts and feelings resulting from this activity, considering the decision and the manner in which it was reached, the behavior of the various participants, and so on. Try to use what you have learned from this book as you share your own opinions and feelings and as you listen to others share theirs.

The negotiation session concludes this chapter, but your school encounters with other adults will, of course, continue. And, as noted earlier, the quality of these encounters rests largely with you, for you are the single most important character in your daily drama, no matter who else is included in the cast.

go!
planning for the present

Recently, I overheard a girl say, "I'm dying to finish high school and start college." I was struck by the use of the words "I'm dying to"; though this odd phrase is commonly used in speaking of strong desires; and I imagined *these* words being uttered by this young person at the close of her life:

> First I was dying to finish high school and start college
> and then I was dying to finish college and start teaching
> and then I was dying to marry and have children

and then I was dying for my children to grow old enough
    for school, so I could return to teaching
and then I was dying to retire
and now I am dying . . .
and I forgot to live.

Living occurs in the here and now and is not something
which can be postponed. If you constantly delay living, the
chances are that you will never live at all. Planning remains a
necessity, however, even though you *must* live in the present,
for if you are to change your teaching life so that it is more satisfying and pleasurable, you must plan—but for the present, not
the future.

The last two activities in this book are included so that
you may assess your teaching and plan to change what you
want to change—now. The first activity is called the Freedom
Scale[1] and the second is a modified force-field analysis, which
we shall call the Action Plan. Both exercises are designed as individual activities; however, it is helpful to share your results with
those of others. If you are not yet a teacher, do the Freedom
Scale and the Action Plan around some other area of your life.

Skill Session 1—The Freedom Scale

Take a sheet of paper and divide it in half. On one side
of the sheet list those behaviors and activities you would like
to institute in your classroom, but which are *expressly forbidden*
to you. On the other side list the behaviors and activities you
would like to institute in your classroom, but which you don't
seem to get to, although no outside force prevents this. Then
compare the length of the two lists and the importance of the
items and assess the amount of freedom which is actually available to you. Use what you learn from this activity in the next
skill session.

[1] I learned this activity from Dr. Herbert Thelen of the University of
Chicago.

Skill Session 2—The Action Plan

Write down your diagnoses and decisions for the following four items:

1. These are behaviors and activities that are part of my teaching, but that I do *not* want to retain:
2. These are behaviors and activities I want to institute or retain in my teaching:
3. These are forces I need to change in order to achieve my teaching goals:
4. Here is what I am going to *do* in order to bring about the desired changes:

Your teaching life, the rest of the story, will be largely written by you. You will be the central character, and even though time, place, events, and other people will have some influence, you will have the greatest impact on the developing plot. Since life is lived in the present, you need to take advantage of the ways open to you to change the here and now, so that each day is more satisfying for you. The remaining chapters will be composed by you, and you will begin as you close the covers of this book.